'I am sure that my father, in his fina
dementia, would have profound]
support that this book describes. ᴎᴇᴌᴇᴎ presents an approach to
counselling older adults that is humanising, compassionate, relationally
deep and informed throughout by theory and her own extensive
clinical experience. It is a unique text that brings to life the reality, and
the potential, of working with this client group. An invaluable read for
counsellors and psychotherapists working in this field.'

**Mick Cooper, Professor of Counselling Psychology,
University of Roehampton**

'*Living Well and Dying Well* is exquisitely written in its depiction of
therapeutic encounters with older adults. Kewell's searingly insightful
and fearlessly honest reflections are at once challenging and inspiring.
The reader not only learns of the interplay between theory and
practice but is invited into the relatively unchartered territory of
psychotherapy with the profoundly old. Rich with personal story,
Living Well and Dying Well salutes old age and explores how we
can engage therapeutically with curiosity and true dignity. This is a
profound, transformative and pioneering piece in the emerging field
of work with older adults. I imagine that, with an ageing population,
the wisdom and beauty held within these pages will only grow in
relevance over time for counsellors and para-professionals alike.'

**Felicity Chapman, clinical social worker and author of
*Counselling and Psychotherapy with Older People in Care:
a support guide***

'This a timely and important book that takes a fresh approach to a
relatively neglected area of counselling and psychotherapy. Writing in
the first person, Helen Kewell provides us with a personal and moving
account of work with a number of clients facing the challenges of later
life. The title refers to "tales of counselling older people". However, this

book is far from anecdotal. The encounters with clients provide the basis for moving inductively to theory and principles, informed by a strong underpinning literature. While the tone is warm and engaging, there is nothing anodyne here. We are challenged to reflect on the social construction of ageing and how the assumptions that can follow from this impinge upon our practice.'

Dr David Bott, Principal Lecturer in Psychotherapy,
University of Brighton

'I loved all these stories, but it was when I came to the one about Kate that I realised I really trusted the author. Few writers would have discussed problems that they could not solve. How often do we write about the painful process of learning to be an effective therapist? This book will help many people become more effective helpers of older and grieving clients.'

Anne Wyatt-Brown, Emeritus Professor in Linguistics,
University of Florida, and former co-editor of the
Journal of Aging, Humanities and the Arts

About the author

Helen Kewell qualified as a humanistic counsellor, having spent most of her previous career as a management consultant – a change that was as necessary as it was dramatic, having experienced loss and chronic illness during the preceding years. During her training, Helen became profoundly influenced by existential and experiential approaches to therapy and, almost inadvertently, became fascinated and inspired by working with older adults. She considers this area of psychotherapeutic work to be under-represented in literature and under-resourced more generally. She hopes to promote a wider dialogue on counselling with older people and to encourage others to do the same. She runs her own private counselling practice in Sussex and continues to volunteer as a counsellor and supervisor for Cruse Bereavement Care.

LIVING WELL AND DYING WELL

TALES OF COUNSELLING OLDER PEOPLE

HELEN KEWELL

First published 2019

PCCS Books Ltd
Wyastone Business Park
Wyastone Leys
Monmouth
NP25 3SR
UK

Tel +44 (0)1600 891509
contact@pccs-books.co.uk
www.pccs-books.co.uk

Living Well and Dying Well: tales of counselling older people

British Library Cataloguing in Publication Data.
A catalogue record for this book is available from the British Library

ISBN 978 1 910919 41 5

Cover design by Jason Anscomb
Printed in the UK by ImprintDigital, Exeter

Dedication

To Irene 'Rene' Goldsmith and Elizabeth 'Betty' Albany – both independent, remarkable, funny, musical, strong-willed women whom I was blessed to call grandmother.

Living Well and Dying Well

Contents

Acknowledgements

This book would never have been written if it weren't for meeting 'Tom'. He is where it all started, and I thank him for inspiring me.

Thanks to my Mum, Anne Albany, for patiently reading every single word I wrote before I sent it to my editor and for understanding what it was I wanted to do, even with no experience in psychotherapy (but with a whole PhD in 'me'). Thank you for getting to know the people in this book through my words and for challenging me and encouraging me in equal measure.

Thanks to Sarah Bailes, my fellow traveller into psychotherapy, who always inspires me to be a better version of my psychotherapeutic self and who constantly believes in me, while quietly, patiently holding my (often considerable) ego in check.

Thank you Sonia, for being my constant and my anchor.

Thanks to Georgia, Lucas and Ethan for their patience while I sat glued to my laptop, surrounded by books, dismissing absent-mindedly their suggestions of other, more exciting things to be doing with our weekends.

Finally, and mostly because he asked me to include him somewhere, thank you to my husband, Nick. He claims to not understand a single word of what I write but reads it anyway and I love him for that. Above all, he has always believed that I can do anything I put my mind to, so he is partly responsible for this book ever being written.

Foreword

Emmy van Deurzen

Working with people who are at the end of their lives is an existential challenge that few of us are fully trained to deal with. It is hard to have real understanding of what happens in the latter years when we ourselves are still at the beginning or the middle of our lives and are preoccupied with very different issues.

This book is a breath of fresh air in that it approaches the stories of people's actual struggles with ageing in a very personal and individual fashion. It shows that when we grow older we are not just 'old people' or 'seniors' or 'elderly'; we continue to be ourselves, with all our memories, our present sensitivities and proclivities and character and with a sense of future that may be foreshortened but that is every bit as important as at any other time of life.

It matters how we approach those final years of our existence. It matters to find someone who can help us reflect on what we regret or what we want to remember and learn from. It matters that we find a way to distil from our lives what is of value and that we transform ourselves into a force for the better for those around us. Passing on our wisdom is certainly a good objective, but before we are ready to do so, there are many personal battles that need first to be won.

Critical self-awareness flows almost directly from our confrontation with the newly wrinkled and less acute version of ourselves that ageing invariably brings. But critical self-awareness can easily turn to resentment and bitterness. The right kind of sensitivity in a counsellor can enable us to find a kinder version of self-reflection that allows us to deal with our memories and recollections of the past in a more constructive fashion.

The many age-related troubles that most of us will have to deal with at a certain time of life sharpen our awareness of mortality. This can lead to self-pity and complaints, instead of guiding us to a ripening into maturity, where we find the right balance between rebellion and acceptance. We know from authors like Simone de Beauvoir (1996) and Lynne Segal (2014) that an attitude of curiosity and defiance may help us stay connected to the world when we are most at risk of withdrawing into solitude and alienation in older age. Engagement with the world and continuing to find a place in it from which we can make our contribution is definitely one of the secrets of successful ageing.

In this book, we are allowed to glimpse into the everyday reality and most private preoccupations of people who are ageing. These stories show us what is actually in the way of a person relaxing into their final decade(s). It also shows how we can help them to face and tackle the challenge of beginning that process of mellowing and ripening.

We still live in a youth-oriented society and it is high time that we turned our attention to the experiences of those who should be honoured, valued and fêted for the experience they have to offer us. We can do much more to enable our elders to share their wisdom, but before we can do this, we have to start paying them proper and careful attention.

Professor Emmy van Deurzen
Principal of the New School of Psychotherapy and Counselling, London and visiting professor with Middlesex University.

References

De Beauvoir S (1996). *The Coming of Age* (P O'Brian, trans). New York, NY: WW Norton & Co.

Segal L (2014). *The Pleasures and the Perils of Ageing*. London: Verso Books.

Introduction

'Then Almitra spoke, saying: We would ask now of death.
And he said:
You would know of death.
But how shall you find it unless you seek it in the heart of life?
The owl whose night-bound eyes are blind until the day cannot
unveil the mystery of light.
If you would indeed behold the spirit of death, open your heart
wide unto the body of life.
For life and death are one, even as the river and the sea are one.'
Kahlil Gibran, *The Prophet*

'Death is known to us simply as the end.'
CG Jung, *The Soul and Death*

In the middle of a particularly frustrating hour of administration and
emails, there it was, the email I had been half-expecting, had partly
prepared for, and that I opened with a tremor of sadness. It was from
the daughter of Maggie, an 80-year-old lady I had been meeting with
for eight months in the care home where she had moved following the
death of her husband. After a brief period of declining health, Maggie
had died quietly in her sleep a few days previously. I felt two parts
of myself respond emotionally in different ways. One part hung my
head, silently wept and allowed myself to grieve a life that had gone,
and the lady, always immaculately dressed and with an infectious but

rare smile, whom I would never see again. The other part felt jubilant, metaphorically looked skywards, imagining Maggie to be floating free of the constrictions of mind and body that had slowly been closing in on her during our time together.

We counsellors cut our teeth on the business of endings; our training begins by considering endings and we begin with our clients by considering endings. Endings are what we do; we are good at this stuff. It wasn't until I began working therapeutically with elderly and profoundly old people that I realised I'd never included death in my litany of possible endings. Yet it is always there as a possibility, whoever one works with.

One of my very first clients was Tom, a 95-year-old man grieving the loss of his wife, with whom I worked at the care home where he lived. I was still training. I was terrified. What could I possibly do to alleviate the distress of a man at the very end of his life? As I went in for our first session, I felt inescapably young, impotent against the tidal wave of grief, ill health, powerlessness and distress that I imagined I would meet. He took each of these presuppositions and turned them on their head. I learnt so much about myself and who I would become as a counsellor within those few weeks. It was a crash course on what it means to experience love and loss within the therapeutic encounter. Above all, it changed the way I view life, ageing and death and, crucially, how to work therapeutically with people who are approaching the end of their lives. This chance referral put me on a course I had never expected.

I passionately believe that, by engaging in counselling, we can liberate ourselves to be all that we are, rather than who we present to the world or the person others want to see. It is an emancipatory and political act, and I often feel, in my role as a counsellor, that I am mounting a tiny insurgence against a world that celebrates certainty and within which people can become socially and culturally boxed, like objects. In this context, I experience my work with those approaching the end of their lives as vibrant and rewarding. Older people can find themselves objectified in society and marginalised in psychotherapy services (Pilgrim, 1997). Writing during her own advancing years, de Beauvoir (1972) proposed that we experience our old age as a reflection of people's reactions to us, often conflicting with how we truly feel inside. My wonderful grandmother, on her 90th birthday, giggled as she exclaimed, wide-eyed: '90! But I don't feel old,

I still feel like I'm in my 20s!' This disconnect between our personal experience of self and the societal and cultural representations of age can cause crisis. As counsellors, our role, as always, is to recognise, encourage and celebrate the unique individuality of our clients and to explore their reality, rather than one constructed by others.

Never was this more important than now. We undoubtedly live in an ageing society. Although only 0.9% of the total UK population in 2015 were more than 90 years old, the size of this age group relative to the rest of the population has increased dramatically in the past 30 years. In 1985, there were 344 people aged 90 and older per 100,000 population; by 2015, this had grown to 854 people per 100,000 population. The Office for National Statistics predicts that the number of people aged 80 and above will double by 2037 and the number of people over 90 will triple (Office for National Statistics, 2017). Taking a global view, in the 20th century more years were added to average life expectancy than all years added in total across the whole of human evolution (Carstensen, 2011).

Despite studies showing that those in older age are more content than the younger population (Carstensen, 2011), there remains within this growing demographic a propensity for poor mental health, as there does in all age categories. Depression affects around 22% of men and 28% of women aged 65 years and over. Yet it is estimated that 85% of older people with depression in the UK receive no help at all from the NHS (Age UK, 2018). One imagines that part of the rationale for this is that society expects a certain amount of depression in older people; it rather goes with the territory, as it were, of experiencing the accumulated losses of career, role, income, good health and friends and partners. Is this OK? Imagine being told, 'Well, I understand that you are depressed but this is natural for your stage of life, there's nothing we can offer to help.' Ridiculous.

I once read an excerpt from Freud's writings where he categorically stated that older people were not able to make effective use of therapy (Hildebrand, 1982). While this point of view is undoubtedly of its time and outdated, I believe it is still held by some. Witness the fact that youth counselling services, although underfunded, are a unique psychotherapeutic offering, but end-of-life counselling is not. It is estimated that dementia in 65–80-year-olds gets much more attention from health professionals than depression in the same age group, despite the fact that depression is twice as prevalent (Pilgrim, 1997).

We don't stop wanting to live successfully, to grow, change or heal, just because we have fewer years ahead of us than behind us – far from it! When Erikson, approaching his own old age, added the final life stage to his developmental theory, he argued that the task for this last stage is about reflection and about integrating past, present and future to find acceptance of the life that has been lived. Indeed, many people find themselves vividly remembering their childhoods and talking about the past as they approach their own death, often with a view to trying to balance the conflicts of those periods (Erikson & Erikson, 1998). I would argue that another task of ageing is to actively challenge long-held life narratives and dare to write new ones, where possible.

It is for all these reasons that counselling for people in their late middle age (65+), elderly people (for our purposes 80+) and the profoundly old (90+) is powerful and important work. And yet it gets very little air time in literature and very little funding. When Erikson published his study on old age with his wife in 1989, the Chicago Tribune said in its review that this was an 'understudied and under-appreciated period of life' (1989). Luckily, the intervening decades have seen much greater leaps in research and attitude towards later life. The very brilliant and compassionate Atul Gawande has single-handedly influenced this in the past five years with his book on mortality (2015), and there are many others. I have provided some further reading and viewing at the end of this book that I have found inspirational. To borrow the words of Bill Thomas (2017), an authority on geriatric medicine and care, and leader of ChangeAging: 'It is in the process of re-examining the lives we have lived, re-evaluating the choices we have made and re-considering the painful feelings that we've always run away from in the past that we eventually find our true selves.' To my mind, if we can learn to live well – that is, to know ourselves, to understand our story and be the author of it – and if we can courageously confront our feelings about our death, then we can die well too.

In what follows, I share the elements I have found to be important when working with this particular client group, brought to life by accounts of the very people who have inspired me. It is important to acknowledge that these accounts will be heavily biased by my experience of these sessions, what interested me about the work with that person, and my reflections and regard towards them that emerged during the writing process. It will also be inescapably influenced by my own experiences of life, loss, ageing and death. I don't apologise for this; it can only be this way, but it needs to be acknowledged.

As I was researching this book and beginning to write, I noticed that, each time I considered growth, meaning-making, development of self and acceptance of death, I physically felt what became a familiar, involuntary fluttering of hope within me. Not to be too critical of myself, this sensation was also a tiny flare of passion for the potential therapeutic journey of the individuals I worked with, rather than simply a salve for my own existential fears of dying: what might they discover and how might they grow? Nevertheless, hope was present, and still is, as I continue to write this book. It leads me to consider whether each of us who chooses to work with elderly people and those at the end of life does so with the wish that we can learn how to approach the end of our own life with a healthy amount of reflection and acceptance. Can supporting or caring for others ever be a selfless act? In her book about supporting dying patients, Byock (1997) talks of the organic nature of community, of its complementary but opposing forces of those who need something and those who provide. She does so in order to help a dying public servant see that he still has a role within his community. Perhaps we who choose to support others rely on those people having needs in order to fulfil our place, and thus the circle completes. In beginning this journey, I challenge myself, as I do you who read these pages, to continue to reflect on this. I may be sitting in the other chair soon enough; how will I be, what will I learn?

One of the few commonalities that a counsellor shares with their client, other than the fact that we are born and we are human, is that we will both one day face death. As with any lived experience, our death will be unique, but the certainty remains that both of us will one day die and that both of us live with an awareness of this. To me, as an existentially-informed therapist, it is vital that I actively explore my own lived experience of ageing and mortality in supervision and personal therapy, and even more so when I am working regularly with elderly clients.

Something important only became evident to me when I was writing this book: none of the clients I worked with appeared to fear death. Some were willing it to come; others were planning actively for what would happen when it did; yet others regarded it with curiosity. None told me they were afraid to die. I have wondered, as the process of writing has invited such reflection, if this might have been influenced by my own way of being. Perhaps I didn't allow space for people to express their fear of death, or make space for it? I can find many rational reasons why the people in this book didn't explore fear of death with me in our time together, but that wouldn't get close enough to what might have been happening. I regard it as work in progress and something I continue to be curious about in my work.

This book comprises a series of accounts of my experiences with elderly and profoundly old clients. I recognise that how we relate to our own old age and that of others comes partly from the stories we hear about ageing. These stories are told in language that is hard-coded into social constructs: into law, social policy and media reporting, to name but a few (Butler, 1990; Viney, 1993). This phenomenon has tended to be discussed in relation to the feminist paradigm by influencers such as Judith Butler. However, it is no less true when discussing old age. Sociologist Laura Carstensen, who has studied ageing over many years writes: 'Even those who mean to advocate for older people often end up describing their situations in the direst language possible, as a way of ensuring our continued sympathy and support' (2011: 5). I am acutely aware, therefore, of my personal responsibility to avoid this trap when writing my accounts and experiences on this subject.

In the following chapters we meet Tom and Maggie, for whom death is very close and whose day-to-day experiencing is insular, private and reduced to a few hours of wakefulness and one room. We meet Cliff, left alone after the death of his partner, lonely and vulnerable, for whom our counselling sessions were as much about having company as anything else. We meet Kate and Alice, who came willingly to counselling but for whom the task of reawakening feelings from long ago and questioning beliefs was too much and, ultimately, not welcome. We meet others, such as Bobby, who valiantly engaged in reassessing and reconstructing his life narrative and found some release. And we meet Susan, who found herself facing a major life transition much earlier than expected and was able to transcend her circumstances and find a new way of living.

I am committed to allowing each personal, unique construct of old age to come forward in the counselling room and I see this as both an individual and a social act. How better to challenge the received ways of thinking about old age than to write down stories that together can begin to challenge the tyranny of generalisations? We all have a responsibility for stories that are told. My wish is that what I have written on these pages honours the unique experiences of the people I have worked with. All these people, and my experience of them, are real. They and, where relevant, their relatives, have given me their consent to write about the times we spent together. Their names and distinguishing details have been changed to protect their anonymity, but the experiences we shared and the impact on my heart and my work are represented here as accurately as possible.

I originally intended to punctuate the chapters of this book by pulling together themes for the reader's consideration. As the work progressed, I was finding these sections hard to write. I decided that, if I were to read this book, I would want to find my own inspiration in its pages. My hope is that its readers are varied in their experiences and reasons for reading and that each will take something very different from it. I do not profess to be an authority; I am simply passionate about sharing my experiences. I hope these accounts provoke thought, start conversations and inspire others who are in close, supportive contact with those who are nearing the end of their natural life, whether you are a counsellor, a carer, a medical professional, a member of a supporting organisation or a family member. At the very end, in the closing section, I have pulled together a few ideas that I hope will be useful take-aways, at least. For now, though, I encourage you to find your own meanings from these accounts, prompted by your reasons for reading them.

Finally, I feel it is important, before we get started, to acknowledge the lack of diversity among the people whose stories are contained in these pages. The people of older age with whom I have had the privilege of working are exclusively white, British and more often female (63%). I have considered, throughout my work, what part I might be playing in this cultural imbalance. My private practice, to date, follows a similar pattern: 65% female, 99% British and 99.5% white. I have concluded that, as I am a white, British female, these factors alone will play a part in influencing the types of clients who choose to work with me. Second, my private practice work mostly comes by word of mouth among either my own network and friendship groups or via clients who, as we have already established, are predominantly from the same demographic group. Third, I live and work in a part of the country with limited cultural diversity.

Women are more likely, for a host of reasons, to need and find counselling. Black people likewise, while disproportionately represented in the acute mental health sector, are far less likely to engage with counselling, for another host of cultural, attitudinal and accessibility reasons (Pilgrim, 1997). My hope is that, by being accepting, non-judgemental and committed to the uniqueness of the clients that come into my room, and by continuing to account for and be aware of any personal prejudice (conscious or not), there will come a time when I can report a more diverse practice.

I was lucky enough to attend a lecture last year given by Ernesto Spinelli, an existential therapist who has written prolifically and beautifully about his work with clients. In the lecture, he spoke passionately about uncertainty, reminding us that, as nothing is true or certain, all we can account for is who we are or what is happening between us and others at this moment in time. He encouraged us to hold lightly any truth statements about our clients that we notice ourselves tempted to make, and to remain uncertain and flexible about what is happening in the counselling room. He told us to invite into our practice the anxiety that this brings. At the end of the lecture, I approached him, nervously, to ask how I, or anyone else, could possibly write about client experiences, as in the writing about an encounter we are inevitably making some truth statement about it. His response didn't help with my anxiety: 'Well, just write it and see where it goes. Don't plan too much, allow for uncertainty and account for it all by being reflective as your writing progresses.' So, I am writing this, and we will see where it goes.

References

Age UK (2018). *Later Life in the United Kingdom, April 2018.* Factsheet. London: Age UK.

Butler JP (1990). *Gender Trouble: feminism and the subversion of identity.* New York, NY: Routledge.

Byock I (1997). *Dying Well*. New York, NY: Riverhead Books.

Carstensen L (2011). *A Long Bright Future*. New York, NY: Broadway Books.

De Beauvoir S (1972). *Old Age*. London: HarperCollins.

Erikson EH, Erikson JM (1998). *The Life Cycle Completed*. New York, NY: WW Norton & Co.

Gawande A (2015). *Being Mortal: illness, medicine and what matters in the end*. London: Profile Books.

Gibran K (1923/1996). *The Prophet*. Ware: Wordsworth Editions.

Hildebrand J (1982). Psychotherapy with older patients. *British Journal of Medical Psychology 55*: 19–28.

Jung CG (1934/2014). The soul and death. In: Read H, Fordham M, Adler G (eds). *CG Jung: The Collected Works vol VIII*. Hove: Routledge (pp3360–3372).

Office for National Statistics (2017). *Measuring National Well-being: insights into loneliness, older people and well-being, 2015*. Newport: ONS. www.ons.gov.uk/peoplepopulationandcommunity/wellbeing/articles/measuringnationalwellbeing/2015-10-01 (accessed 8 November 2018).

Pilgrim D (1997). *Psychotherapy and Society*. London: Sage Publications.

Thomas B (2017). *Gerotranscendence*. [Blog.] ChangingAging. https://changingaging.org/aging101/gerotranscendence/ (accessed 8 November 2018).

Viney L (1993). *Life Stories*. Chichester: Wiley.

How to say goodbye
Maggie

'Then you and I should bid good-bye for a little while?'
'I suppose so, sir.'
'And how do people perform that ceremony of parting, Jane?'
Charlotte Bronte, *Jane Eyre*

Maggie was just 16 when she went to Whitstable on a day trip with the Bromley Girls Brigade. On the beach, she met John, two years older than her, a soldier on leave. By the end of the day, they were courting; not long afterwards, they were married. When I met Maggie she was 79, living in a care home. Her beloved John had died a few months earlier. He had been the centre of her life and, in the last few years, her only carer. Her family had contacted me as they were worried about how she was coping with the loss of her husband, her independence and her home. She was evidently very upset but had felt unable to talk about it with her close family, or anyone else.

Her family wanted to meet me and were keen to know if I thought counselling would help. Maggie suffered from memory loss due to a series of strokes and had a heart condition that meant her breathing was laboured. They wanted to ensure I was happy that Maggie would be able to cope with the physical and mental demands of counselling. What was, perhaps, left unsaid was, 'Is this a worthwhile investment? Will Mum be able to get anything out of it?' What counsellor would be able to answer that question were it to be posed? We had agreed that

I would visit Maggie, introduce myself and see how our first meeting went. This first occasion of meeting the family and going in to meet Maggie felt like a rather stilted job interview. I remember walking down the corridor to Maggie's room trying to centre myself a little and focus on the one thing that mattered here: a coming together of two human beings and the potential for something healing to happen as a result. Not for the first time in the course of my work with Maggie, it was difficult to hold onto this.

In my experience, the triangular relationship between family, client and counsellor needs to be held carefully, reflected on and actively talked about, to ensure everything that happens is in the service of the person I am counselling. This is true, regardless of the age of the client. The challenge of working in an organisational setting such as a care home, or at the request of concerned family members who are paying for counselling for a loved one, is how to maintain the contact needed to complete the work without inadvertently, or otherwise, betraying confidences or skipping around the client's consent. Usually, I email the person who has initiated the counselling relationship – in this case, Maggie's children – to let them know the session has taken place and to deal with any practical matters such as payment or confirming the next session. As when working in schools or with the parents of a child client, it is incredibly important and difficult in equal measure to tread the line between a simple transaction and the weight of the emotional or political agenda. I am often asked via email how I found my client that day, whether they were able to open up, whether they seemed better. I would never respond to such questions from the relatives of a younger adult client who had engaged me themselves. Yet situations where someone is, if you like, commissioning the work seem to allow this sort of dialogue to creep in. Holding steady against this is important and requires strength.

And it isn't only family members that assume it is their right to enquire. 'How is Maggie today?' the receptionist would say to me as I left the care home, in the same well-meaning, sing-song voice that she reserved for residents and concerned family members. She would continue with a statement such as: 'She's ever so quiet. I think her chest pains are getting worse and she just won't come and join with everyone when we play bingo. I think it would be a lot better for her if she did, don't you?' Can you imagine bumping into and having that same conversation with a friend of an adult client who initiated contact herself and comes independently each week to see you in your private counselling room? It goes against the counsellor's code of ethics; not only that, it flies in the face of the received understanding of what a counselling relationship is about. I often wonder what makes it OK for people to talk this way about the elderly and infirm. It has a lot of parallels with how children are spoken about – as if we know better than them.

The right way to answer this is, of course, along the lines of, 'Yes, I saw Maggie today, but I can't discuss what we talk about as I am bound by counsellor/client confidentiality and it wouldn't be right. I'm sorry.' However, something about the environment seduces even the strongest willed counsellor to the point of disclosure when in its colonising, proprietorial embrace.

Urie Bronfenbrenner (1993) developed a model of human development that describes five socially-organised sub-systems that influence all human beings over their life cycle and help to support human growth: microsystem (family, friends, immediate environment such as schools); mesosystem (where two of these environments intersect, such as parents and school); exosystem (where two or more environments intersect and where one of them has an external influence, not connected to the individual, such as governing bodies or external policies and procedures); macrosystem (wider cultural, social and political influences), and, finally, chronosystem (influence of historical, time-sensitive factors).

Although originally researched and conceptualised to support educational environments, it is, in my experience, a very useful model when considering growth and barriers to growth in any counselling client, whatever their age. In particular, it is a helpful model when working with clients within organisational settings or with other service providers involved in the person's care, or where there is likely to be some level of family intervention, such as with children or older adults. I find that considering these five elements allows me to hold myself steady and authentic and keep focused on the individual in front of me, and to notice but not surrender to the pull and influence of these systems.

Returning to my regular encounters with the receptionist, for example, the care home is both part of the mesosystem within which Maggie and I exist and part of the exosystem, the wider care home group and organisation, which has its own set of procedures, ways of doing things, culture, language and demeanour towards its residents. My role as Maggie's counsellor was to notice this and not to become part of that pattern; to treat her as a unique individual and certainly not as someone to be discussed with all and sundry and cajoled into 'cheering up'.

When I was training and exploring the theoretical frameworks that underpin counselling, I remember reading a dog-eared copy of RD Laing's *The Divided Self* and being moved to tears by his passionate stance against the medical, deterministic model that sees people as objects to be arrogated by diagnosis, and by his call for the therapeutic encounter to value the wholeness of a person (Laing, 1960). Laing wanted therapists to respond to the unique behaviour created by both client and therapist together, in the moment, rather than fixing ourselves to a diagnostic model that perpetuates the person's alienation, disempowerment and distress.

For me, with Maggie, this started even as I entered the care home premises and signed my name in the visitors' book at reception.

I'll paint more of a picture of the environment to illustrate this further. Invariably, when I arrived at the home, the residents would be gathered in the communal lounge, having had their lunch not long before. Usually the television would be on loud or there would be dance-hall music coming from a stereo. Most of the residents would be sitting or dozing in comfortable chairs; some might be playing board games or participating in organised activities at a table at the far end of the room. The air would be warm, stuffy and thick with unsaid words: carers patiently helping residents to play, their minds elsewhere, or trying to maintain patience and compassion despite their own tiredness or frustration; residents frowning in confusion or looking around in wide-eyed surprise at finding themselves here, unable to comprehend how it had come to this, or angry with their bodies for letting them down. Somewhere in this scene, I would see Maggie's familiar pink slippers, then her legs and then her sunken body, bent over, sleeping in her wing-back chair.

Our first task together was to negotiate moving her to her room, where we could have some privacy for our session. If entering the communal room hadn't fully immersed me within the cultural embrace of the care home setting, this experience certainly did. I'd been advised that Maggie should walk to her room, rather than use a wheelchair, as it was good for her continuing mobility to walk a little every day. The problem was that, due to her poor health, she found this process exhausting and distressing. It took two members of staff to lift her upright so she was leaning on her frame, and the four of us then shuffled through the room, out into the corridor and along the 15 metres or so to her room and manoeuvred her into her chair. Throughout the 10 minutes or so that this took, her carers encouraged her with bright, upbeat phrases about how well she was doing.

Never did I feel so out of place (perhaps my own issues were emerging about not being able to help) or so judged by the staff. I did not join in with the 'well dones' and the 'not far to go nows', as I could plainly see the exhaustion and frustration on Maggie's face. When we finally sat facing each other, it felt important that I acknowledge what was happening by being in her exhaustion with her, allowing her to express it and acknowledging this lived experience. Each time I would notice a pull within me to make her more comfortable, to ask if she needed anything and to continue the helping dialogue. 'This is not my role,' I would remind myself; my role is to be with her in her experience, however uncomfortable.

Care homes have good, caring people working in them; they are designed to facilitate a happy life for residents, to support and care for them. Many residents, and their relatives, have no other option once living independently at home is no longer possible for them. Most elderly people still at home are cared for by their partners (some 1.4 million carers in the UK are aged over 65 (Age UK, 2018)). However, while care homes do not take the bulk of the responsibility for care of the elderly infirm (only 14.8% of people age 85+ live in a care or nursing home (Age UK, 2018)), they do tend to be where older people die. The median time between admission to a care home and death is 15 months (Age UK, 2018). Thus, they carry a considerable responsibility.

Try as they might, it is very hard for care home staff to allow residents to live authentically. In *Being Mortal*, a wonderful, ground-breaking book about death, Atul Gawande (2015) advocates passionately for nursing homes that respond to the individual needs of residents, rather than pursue societal or organisational goals. Mostly, activities in caring institutions are, in a word, institutional – organised group activities that have some kind of evidence base for their therapeutic benefits, with residents cajoled into taking part. Meals are made and served up to everyone at the same time every day, regardless of individual hunger or tastes. Residents who choose to stay in their rooms or refuse to eat at the allotted time are considered either to be not coping well or to be trouble-makers; socialising in the communal areas is praised as a sign of psychological good health.

As we approach the end of our life and fully confront and accept its limits, taking a philosophical view of our suffering and death affords an opportunity to find personal growth and meaning. In Erikson's model, the task for the final developmental stage of life is to experience our historical continuity of existence and crown our whole experience – to reflect upon it while acknowledging the painful reality that it is coming to an end (Erikson & Erikson, 1998). As Dylan Thomas wrote so powerfully (1952/2003), 'Old age should burn and rave at close of day.' My own practice is informed by existential approaches and I find this a powerful way of being with clients who are very old or at the end of life. Existential counselling is a philosophical investigation, one that aims to understand life by exploring its boundaries and its possibilities (van Deurzen-Smith, 1988).

Maggie seemed to be pre-programmed to not talk to me about things that were difficult or below the surface. At the beginning of each session, I would ask her what was going on for her in that moment. She'd lift her chin from her clavicle, where it often rested, fix her eyes on me and, registering who I was, smile her bright smile and say something like, 'Oh, I'm OK today, thank you, yes.' Encouraging people to make full contact with pain of loss and fear of death never feels easy, but it is even harder to navigate with those who are elderly, vulnerable and perhaps cognitively impaired. Who wouldn't want to stop at 'I'm OK' and talk about the weather and how nice their hair looks?

Gawande references extensive research showing that terminally ill patients admitted into palliative care, where death is actively talked about, tend to live longer than in hospital environments that focus on keeping people alive. The conclusion is clear: not playing down or ignoring the reality of death can prolong life (Gawande, 2015). From an existential rather than medical standpoint, we would say the same: individualisation and growth continues right up to and on considering our death (van Deurzen-Smith, 1988). If Victor Frankl, writing from a concentration camp where there was nothing else to consider apart from survival and death, could find meaning and growth in this experience, those of us who enjoy relative freedom can surely do the same (Frankl, 1977). By avoiding the realities of our situation, both immediate and existential, we aren't perhaps fully being ourselves. Tolstoy's Ivan Ilyich is in psychological agony for most of the story, while his family and his doctors keep up the pretence that all will soon be well. The moment those around him begin to accept his death, he does too and 'instead of death there was light' (Tolstoy, 1882/2008).

Seen through this lens, I considered it my responsibility to Maggie to find a way into her lived experiences by both of us metaphorically breaking free of the trappings of the mesosystem around her.

I started by noticing what I was seeing, rather than replying to her 'I'm OK' with an equally light response like, 'Oh good!'

Instead, I said: 'You are looking at my shoes and you seem far away in thought, you are shaking your head slowly, Maggie.'

Bringing Maggie into her body and the space between us usually brought about eye contact. Many of Maggie's responses were quite slow, due to the strokes she had experienced, so this eye contact was usually prolonged and intense, and I was careful to hold it and tried to regulate my breathing with hers where possible. This wasn't a deliberate technique but seemed to help me tune into her rhythm and pace. One of the first times this happened, after a long interval, Maggie's face crumpled and she turned to the photo next to her and said, 'I miss my John' and wept. We had moved quite quickly from 'OK' to grief, simply by being present in our bodies.

This was the pattern of most of our sessions. Sometimes Maggie was too tired to talk with any regularity of back-and-forth conversation. I drew heavily on pre-therapy approaches at these times, using simple word repetition and mirroring actions to maintain contact at even a most basic level (Prouty, Portner & Werde, 2002). Once I gently eased myself onto a cushion on the floor as Maggie seemed to be struggling to hold up her head to make any eye contact. This worked well in that session; mostly it was trial and error, sometimes getting it wrong. What guided me was staying with whatever was going on for Maggie that day, letting her know I was there and trying not to direct her but feel into places that felt important.

One day she was absent-mindedly fingering a necklace around her neck. I reflected this back to her and then, when she looked puzzled, I held a mirror to it for her to see it. She told me that John had given it to her for her 21st birthday 'a few weeks ago'. This conversation led her to talk to me about how angry she was at him being away so much for his work, leaving her alone in Bromley. She cried for him, telling me how painful it was to be alone. I felt these could be memories from his time in the military when they were newly married but the parallels with her loss now seemed important. Simone de Beauvoir (1972) noted that that we relive unpleasant memories in later life so that we can process and reflect on them. I wondered if making contact with her anger and disappointment at him leaving her then somehow felt healing now, when she was feeling abandoned and lonely in a care home, having had to leave her own home after John died.

On other days, Maggie would be more awake, more in the present. At these times we encountered together her experience of her advancing years. As we meandered through dialogue about the weather ('so hot at the moment!'), the Turkish delight in the bowl next to her (her favourite treat) and the roses at her bedside, received for her recent birthday, I asked about her age. 'I think I'm 80,' she said tentatively. The card indeed said that, so we read the messages in it together and she cried out very suddenly, as if physically hurt, 'Oh! I'm 80! But I'm so old, I don't want to be old!' Her face contorted into one of such pain and her eyes darted around as if seeing the room for the first time: a folded wheelchair in the corner, a sink with a handle on it for stability, a bed with bars that could be raised for safety, the wipe-clean cushion she was sitting on, the red button strung permanently around her neck to push in emergencies. At this moment I felt an involuntary flex of the culturally-learned response to minimise or dismiss her assertion that she was 'so old'.

We hear it said so often: 'Oh no, you don't look a day over 50; you look incredible for your age,' or, 'You have years left in you, don't be silly!' It's all around us in social discourse, reflected in the media in products advertised as 'age-defying'. Contemporary Western society honours youth over old age and sees vitality and physical strength as the most dignified way of being (Byock, 1997). De Beauvoir (1972), writing in her advancing years, maintained that we experience old age through internalising other people's reactions to us that are starkly at odds with how we feel about ourselves.

Added to this, we now have more old people than young people globally than at any time in recorded history (Carstensen, 2011), meaning that taking care of older people could place a burden on the younger people and, crucially, that each old person has less perceived value in society. This is in stark contrast to traditional societies where older people are usually the leaders and most revered for their extensive knowledge about politics, medicine, religion, songs and dances (Diamond, 2013).

How do we counsellors liberate elderly clients from this usual way of relating? I regard the potential gift of a therapeutic encounter to be the presence of another person who experiences you for all you are and explores what this means, rather than fitting you into categories. Identity cannot be categorised, as it is relational and historically situated, created by an ever-evolving and ongoing dialogue (Butler, 1990). Therefore, to me, our role as counsellors is to introduce possibility and emancipate clients from 'the usual' way of relating. Indeed, research has borne out that the progression of dementia can be slowed if those caring for people with the condition relate to them and emphasise their individuality and unique identity, rather treating them purely as someone with dementia (Greenfield, 2008). By introducing the possibility of a different way of relating within the microcosm of the therapeutic dyad, we can challenge the experience in the macrocosm of the rest of the world (Bronfenbrenner, 1993).

I tried to hold myself steady in those moments by simply noticing what was pulling me to minimise her experience of her age and by staying focused on Maggie, her lived experience of her age and what she was trying to express. I reflected to her that it seemed distressing for her to consider her age in that moment, and I asked her what it meant to her to be 80.

'Oh well, it means I am old, I'm going to die soon,' she replied.

'That feels hard to think about,' I offered.

'Hmm.' Here Maggie's gaze drifted off beyond me to the photographs on the shelves to the right of me. The tiniest trace of a frown came onto her face and she narrowed her eyes.

I followed her gaze. 'Are you looking at these photos?' I asked.

Maggie reached out her hand towards them and I asked if she'd like me to lift them down.

'That's my Mum on that side,' and she pointed to a tiny, framed, black-and-white photo of a lady in a wool suit and hat. 'And the one on the other side is my Dad,' she finished, gesturing to another black-and-white photograph of a man in a white t-shirt, arm raised to shield his eyes from the sun. I took them both down from the shelf and gently placed them on the bedside table to her right. She looked at them and reached out to touch them in turn.

'Can you tell me about them?' I asked.

'Oh, I loved them very much. I miss them... I wonder what they think of me now, in here.' Maggie paused to look around: 'If they think I've done alright in my life.'

There seemed to be a strong connection between considering her own advancing age and approaching death and her experience of her parents.

Later, at her funeral, I learned that Maggie had moved her parents near to her as they grew older and cared for them both as much as she could. Perhaps her advancing age and death took her full circle to being someone's daughter, dependent and vulnerable.

When language and conversation grew difficult, as it often did, due to Maggie's tiredness, we looked around the room and I asked her about the other people whose photos were on the shelves. As we toured around these photos, there seemed to be a circularity of experience as Maggie talked to me about her own daughters and grandchildren. She often found it difficult to remember their names and their relation to her. I tried hard not to correct her; accuracy didn't feel as important as the connections between the pictures and her feelings. Sometimes she smiled broadly; at other times she frowned. This all felt like a meaningful connection for her between her experience, that of her parents and the love of her wider family.

She appeared less distressed than usual but nonetheless thoughtful and quiet as I left her that day. I was reminded of the Nietzsche quote I'd read in Frankl's tiny, powerful book (1977: 84): 'He who has a why to live for can bear any how.' It felt as though we had moved from dying to the love of family and within that there was both comfort and meaning.

However, it would be untrue to look at our work together through rose-tinted spectacles. Some of it did appear to be healing, but there were many times when it was awkward or difficult. After Maggie spent some time in hospital with pneumonia, her daughters asked her if she'd like me to continue visiting, to which she'd consented. There were times during our subsequent sessions when Maggie fell asleep as we sat in silence. This presented me, a relatively inexperienced counsellor, with a dilemma. We had already reduced the length of the sessions to 30 minutes, in discussion with Maggie and with her daughters, as I felt the effort of talking one-on-one over a sustained period was very tiring for Maggie. If a client sleeps through a session that they are paying for, is this ethically OK? What if a client sleeps through a session someone else is paying for? Does that change things? Ethically, I subscribe to never exploiting a client, and this felt close to financial exploitation if I was merely sitting while my client dozed (BACP, 2018).

Supervision helped me get more comfortable with this. I felt I wasn't doing anything in those times, so the client and her family were not getting their money's worth, as it were, from me. I wondered whether the initial conversation with Maggie's family had allowed me to interject an expectation on their part that I would somehow 'fix' Maggie. Once we'd identified this, my supervisor encouraged me to go back to basics: to centre myself back within my theoretical frame and the fundamentals of my practice. As a practitioner, two things matter to me: being fearlessly phenomenological by noticing and responding to the present moment, and to journey alongside a client's lived experience. Nothing in either of these elements of my practice encourages me to 'do stuff' or 'give the client their money's worth'. So how did I balance my ethical foundations with my beliefs about my practice?

I found the answer in both. As Maggie's eyelids fluttered closed one day, I leaned in and gently said: 'Maggie, I notice you seem very tired today.'

A slow nod, with closed eyes.

'It feels like talking with me today is making you more tired.'

No response, her eyes remained closed.

'I wonder if it would be better for you if we left it for today and I came back another time, Maggie?'

On this occasion she opened her eyes, squinted a little in looking for me and, when she found my eyes, said very slowly: 'I like you being here.'

I paused and nodded. Then I asked her: 'What it is like for you when I am here?'

There was a long pause, so long that I thought she had returned to sleep. Then she said, simply: 'Safe.'

I stayed with her for the 10 minutes that remained while she dozed. It felt OK. I have since reflected on this experience through the lens of Buber's theory of 'I-Thou'. He wrote that the 'thou' relation between two people is below language, pre-verbal as it were (Morgan-Williams, 2002). I feel Maggie and I experienced this together in those moments. I believe that, as death approaches, we can experience a reversal of Lacan's mirror (Lacan, 1980). Lacan theorises that, as new-borns, we resolve our sense of fragmentation by seeing our wholeness reflected in those who care for us. So too, I would argue, the close attention of another helps prevent the fragmentation of self and confusion that can be experienced in profoundly old age.

In focusing only on what was happening and what it was like for Maggie, even in those simple terms, I was staying true to my practice. However, I also kept us focused on Maggie's autonomy and choice. She and I were within an environment where residents' autonomy is contained within certain limits. Ours is also a society that has a collective view of elderly people and what is right or wrong for them. The best I could do was focus wholeheartedly on her experience and choice in our moments together.

Maggie died peacefully after we had been meeting for about nine months, following a short stay in hospital. We were to take a few weeks' break from our sessions over the summer holidays. When I left at the end of the final session before the break, deep inside I sensed I wouldn't see her again. Our sessions, as I said, had become introspective and quiet, and I noticed Maggie was turning towards herself and away from the world around her. I asked if I could return in three weeks, as I always did at the end of a session. She squeezed her eyes shut and nodded firmly and slowly, then opened her eyes and smiled at me. I remember leaning in and squeezing her hand and saying 'Goodbye' before leaving the room. I quietly wept as I walked the familiar route along the corridor and down the stairs, signed out and climbed into my car.

During our three-week break, Maggie was taken to hospital, then returned to the home for respite care before slipping away and dying in her sleep. Her family were kind enough to let me know. I asked if there was a way I could pay my respects that felt comfortable for them and received an open invitation to the funeral and wake in return. This was the first funeral of a client that I had attended. I had experienced the death of another client, but had no contact with his relatives, having worked only with and through the care home, so was not able to find out where the funeral was taking place or where his ashes were laid. His family remained as elusive after his death as they had been in his memory during our time together. I had found this difficult and was therefore grateful for the opportunity to say goodbye to Maggie.

I realise that this chapter is a strange, perhaps bleak way to open a book. My editor would rather I didn't. In itself, what Maggie and I experienced together doesn't constitute an empowering, uplifting account. However, I am an existentially informed therapist and talk of dying and death is my currency. Death is part of life. It is a given. Why not start with it? In the closing chapter of her memoirs, Diana Athill reflects that it is not possible to end such a book with a 'bang'. Perhaps it is not possible to begin a book about therapeutic work with those who are nearing the end of life without talking about death. Athill perceptively writes:

> From up here, I can look back and see that, although human life is less than the blink of an eyelid in terms of the universe, within its own framework, it is amazingly capacious. One life can contain serenity and tumult, heartbreak and happiness, coldness and warmth, grabbing and giving. (2008: 177)

Human life is a question of opposites: death allows us to reflect on life and, if we are brave enough, life allows us to reflect on death. That is why the title of this book focuses on both.

And so, I found myself attending Maggie's funeral. Is there a kind of hierarchy of grievers at a funeral? Until then I had only ever attended funerals of family members. I had been so swept along by grief, reflection and my own thoughts on those occasions that I had never noticed or thought about these dynamics. As I travelled there, I noticed how nervous I was, how unsure of how to act, how to strike the right balance of reverence of the occasion and allow myself to grieve and find my goodbye. I was mentally preparing myself not to lose control completely. My tears are very unpredictable, even at the best of times – what if I were to cry too much? I found myself struggling to get a sense of how much emotion was appropriate for the counsellor of the person who had died, as if there were some accepted scale of sadness.

At some point before the start of the service, I noticed that I was trying to intellectually organise the experience in my head instead of feeling into the occasion with authenticity. Where would I sit? What should I say if someone asked me who I was and how I knew Maggie? Should I approach the grieving family at the end? Tuning into these reflections within the moment can be so helpful, like an inner supervisory voice (Bager-Charleson, 2010). In the end, I surmised, what did it matter? As the celebrant eloquently put it, we were all there because our lives were touched by Maggie in some way; my only task today was to make my own goodbye in the way that felt appropriate.

What I wasn't prepared for was the eulogistic speech made by the celebrant, the family having chosen not to give one. As the ceremony unfolded, she gave a life history, facts of Maggie's life, if you will, provided by the family. In what other situation would a counsellor be provided with a factual timeline of their client's life? I felt myself resenting this intrusion into our work together, into my memories of her and the meaning of what she had chosen to reveal through our sessions.

Maggie's memories were muddled towards the end of our time together but, as with any work with individuals with dementia or cognitive impairment, the content is not what is important; rather, what matters is the process or the clues to the client's experiences that are revealed and afford opportunity for meaning-making. On one occasion, after a period of silence spent looking at the chair opposite, Maggie raised her eyebrows in surprise. When I reflected this back to her, she said: 'I think I got married this week.' We explored together what had happened – she had married someone other than John, but John had given her his blessing. She said she couldn't be sure if it really happened but that it felt real. As we explored it further, she told me John was happy for her to move on and she smiled a faraway smile. The facts of the situation were entirely irrelevant but the meaning was vital.

As the eulogy progressed, I found myself stacking up everything we had talked about and putting it into categories of real versus fantasy. Then I caught myself: why was this important? In some ways, it felt like the moment you chance on a client in the supermarket with their family and find yourself involuntarily comparing what you see with what they have told you in the work. In some ways, my internal process was helpful; it left me in the end with acceptance that what Maggie and I shared in our sessions was important at the time. Like a photograph taken on a certain day, with a certain type of weather, at a certain time, the same view will look completely different to someone else who visits in a different season, at a different time, in different weather. There is no truth to the matter, only meaning.

References

Age UK (2018). *New analysis shows number of older people with unmet care needs soars to record high*. Press release. London: Age UK. www.ageuk.org.uk/latest-press/articles/2018/july-2018/new-analysis-shows-number-of-older-people-with-unmet-care-needs-soars-to-record-high/ (accessed 8 November 2018).

Athill D (2008). *Somewhere Towards the End*. London: Granta.

BACP (2018). *Ethical Framework for the Counselling Professions*. Lutterworth: BACP. www.bacp.co.uk/events-and-resources/ethics-and-standards/ethical-framework-for-the-counselling-professions (accessed 1 December 2018).

Bager-Charleson S (2010). *Reflective Practice in Counselling and Psychotherapy*. London: Sage Publications.

Bronfenbrenner U (1993). Ecological models of human development. In: Gauvain M, Cole M (eds). *Readings on the Development of Children*. New York, NY: Freeman (pp37–43).

Bronte C (1847/1992). *Jane Eyre*. Ware: Wordsworth Editions.

Butler JP (1990). *Gender Trouble: feminism and the subversion of identity*. New York, NY: Routledge.

Byock I (1997). *Dying Well: peace and possibilities at the end of life*. New York, NY: Riverhead Books.

Carstensen L (2011). *A Long Bright Future*. New York, NY: Broadway Books.

De Beauvoir S (1972). *Old Age*. London: HarperCollins.

Diamond J (2013). *How Societies Can Grow Old Better*. [Video.] TED2013. www.ted.com/talks/jared_diamond_how_societies_can_grow_old_better (accessed 8 November 2018).

Erikson EH, Erikson JM (1998). *The Life Cycle Completed*. New York, NY: WW Norton.

Frankl VE (1977). *Man's Search for Meaning: an introduction to logotherapy*. New York, NY: Pocket Books.

Gawande A (2015). *Being Mortal: illness, medicine and what matters in the end*. London: Profile Books.

Greenfield S (2008) *ID: the quest for meaning in the 21st century*. London: Hodder & Stoughton.

Lacan J (1980). *Ecrits: a selection* (A Sheridan, trans). London: Tavistock Publications.

Laing RD (1960). *The Divided Self: an existential study in sanity and madness*. London: Tavistock Publications.

Morgan-Williams S (2002). All real living is meeting. In: du Plock S (ed). *Further Existential Challenges to the Psychotherapeutic Theory and Practice: papers from Existential Analysis*. London: Society for Existential Practice (pp105–123).

Prouty GF, Portner M, Van Werde D (2002). *Pre-therapy: reaching contact-impaired clients*. Ross-on-Wye: PCCS Books.

Thomas D (1952/2003). Do not go gentle into that good night. In: Jones D (ed). *The Poems of Dylan Thomas*. New York, NY: New Directions Publishing.

Tolstoy L (1882/2008). *The Death of Ivan Ilyich and Other Stories*. Harmondsworth: Penguin Classics.

Van Deurzen-Smith E (1988). *Existential Counselling in Practice*. London: Sage Publications.

Rewriting narratives
Bobby

'If you look for truth, you may find comfort in the end.'
CS Lewis, *Mere Christianity*

'As if there could be true stories: things happen in one way, and
we retell them in the opposite way.'
Jean-Paul Sartre, *Nausea*

We all recognise the stereotype of the elderly person recounting
stories of the good old days when they were young to anyone who will
listen. Outside the counselling room, we might also admit to a slightly
distracted, eye-rolling response to tales that are often repetitive and
obsessed with the past. However, as with any content that is brought
to counselling, these stories hold clues to a client's process, how they
are in the world and what might be healing and helpful for them; they
are not to be dismissed. In her book on narrative therapy with elderly
people, Linda Viney extols the power of reconstructing life stories
in therapy as a way of strengthening self-hood at a time of constant
change, of sequencing the complexity of a long life and, more broadly,
as a way of empowering a demographic group whose stories are often
told for them or about them (1993).

Bobby was a 79-year-old man I worked with for six months,
following the death of his wife to whom he'd been married for 55 years.
Scottish, talkative and hard of hearing, Bobby greeted me each week at

his house wearing a flat cap and an ancient pair of silk pyjamas under his clothes to keep out the cold. The story of his life, as it unfolded, was one of poverty, adversity and sheer bloody-minded hard work. He retold it from many angles, week after week, and always cast himself as a bad man who made poor choices and was undeserving of his wife's love while she was alive, so didn't deserve to grieve for her after her death.

Following his wife's death, Bobby had found himself the reluctant patriarch of a large and complicated family of whom he was, mostly, fond, despite his disappointment with how some members chose to live their lives. He was often lonely but he reached out to them in the best way he could, giving them money every now and then and learning how to send messages on his iPad, which he was very proud to show me. He also took care of other elderly relatives by phoning and sending gifts when he could. He fed milk to stray cats in his garden. He didn't like to go out on his own but, from his small, red-brick council house, where he had lived for most of his married life, he did what he could to look out for others and maintain his sense of having a place in the world.

I enjoy talking; it is of no surprise to me or to those who know me that I chose a profession that uses words and feelings as its currency. I find inspiration for my clinical practice from an existential approach to therapy that invites clients into an active, reflective exploration of their world. Of course, one of the philosophical underpinnings of existential therapy is Socrates, who encouraged a dialectic debate, using challenge to liberate people to find awareness of themselves in the world. As Plato has Socrates say in his dialogue *Theaetetus* (369BCE/2014): 'Wonder is the beginning of wisdom.' I am also drawn to the courage, creativity and moment-to-moment attention that creates the 'safe emergency' of the Gestalt approach (Perls, 1969). For me, therapy is about both client and therapist being alive and present within the encounter, pushing gently but insistently at the door of client experience (Mearns & Cooper, 2005). It's about being alive to what is happening between us in the therapeutic dyad, wondering about it, being aware of inconsistencies or themes within a client's narrative and noticing and communicating back its effect on me as it unfolds. I learnt much about the power of this approach through my work with Bobby.

I will focus in fine detail on a few minutes of the many hours I spent with Bobby in order to bring to life the power of staying very present and phenomenologically focused when life narratives are being explored. I worked with Bobby during my original training and recorded our sessions, with his consent, as part of my ongoing development, which means I have been able to focus in detail on the second-by-second unfolding of our encounter. These few moments I will explore here were the most significant of our work together – both for him, as he later told me, and for me. They have powerfully influenced how I work today and, I believe, say something useful about how we can all orientate ourselves towards each other.

RD Laing asks us to orientate ourselves with plasticity towards the other person in the room, to use our relatedness in each moment for therapeutic ends (1960). This need not be any different with an older client: we need not necessarily assume any vulnerability due to age that precludes our taking an active, phenomenological approach to the stories people bring to therapy. The expansion of the narrative of our life and the development of selfhood never ceases. The theory of gerotranscendence, developed over a 20-year period by Lars Tornstam, challenged the received way of conceptualising later life as a time for continuity and preserving mid-life ideals and definitions of reality (Tornstam, 1997). Gerotranscendence adopts a contrasting perspective that emphasises solitude, change and growth. This became useful for me to hold in mind when working with Bobby.

Before we explore my time with Bobby further, it is important to note that, to enable this pliability of selfhood – this flexibility towards life narrative – to happen with our clients, a counsellor must be prepared to do the same. When I first came to counselling, I was bound by a limiting belief that I might be too facilitative to be an effective humanistic counsellor (I'd previously spent 17 years working in an industry that specialises in high-energy problem-solving and fixing, and these were hard habits to break). Through my personal therapy over the years, I have come to find acceptance for all parts of myself, including the part I used to negatively conceptualise as 'The Beast', which drove me to habitually over-organise and over-achieve, and which ultimately resulted in my physical breakdown in 2012. It took a while for me to see that it was holding me back to hang onto my story that this part of me was negative and that the softer, feeling part of me was positive. It seems obvious now that this way of relating to myself was limiting me, in that it offered only two ways to respond to life. I had created a fixed selfhood through the story I told myself about my life.

My counsellor was the first of us to offer compassion to 'The Beast' and to notice that this part of me was as necessary as any other and had served me well. Together, we considered the many shades of grey between the black/white, good/bad that I identified within myself. Challenging that story and reflecting on experiences with clients in supervision enabled me to allow all parts of myself to work together and to trust that this can happen in the service of the client. Spinelli (2002) urges us to fully be ourselves when we encounter our clients and to use all that we are, including our own experiences as a client. Likewise, research has shown that a therapist's personal therapy allows for a much deeper developmental journey in our work (Phillips, 2011). This continuous journey of acceptance through both personal therapy and supervision has allowed me to feel more comfortable about turning up at my clients' front doors, and my hope is that it enables me to meet them more fully as a result.

How else could I attempt to explore fluidity of self with clients, especially those who have had many more years of finding and fixing life narratives? As I have mentioned, Bobby was a story-teller. He loved DVD box sets of historical dramas and, despite having had limited education in his early years, read avidly. He saw themes and similarities between what he read and watched and often started our sessions talking about this and then interpreting his life within its context. We frequently meandered through accounts of World War Two veterans, criminal profiling and stories of Greek gods, to arrive finally at some personal meaning. Unlike many of the people of his generation I have worked with, Bobby talked relatively openly and with insight about his feelings about what had happened to him. His memories were sharp and crystal clear in detail.

I had noticed a tendency in our sessions for Bobby to reject any reflections I made of him doing something kind or good. This seemed to be a strongly held, persistent response, but I felt it was wearing thin, even for him. At the start of the extract that I am about to examine in detail, I had just pulled together what he had told me about helping various members of his family and had reflected back how different this construction felt to the more familiar narrative about him being a difficult, rude man.

'I sense that, when I say to you that you, that your family do like you, do want you, that you are helping them... that you can't take that in... and feel it.'

Here I emphasised the word 'in' while holding my hand to my chest, to try to bring us into the feeling of the moment, rather than a cognitive response.

'No, I – I – I can't, I can't.' Bobby shook his head and continued, almost involuntarily: 'No, because I feel I've been... I've always been a bit tight fisted. It was only because we came up from such a hard sort of... what do you call it...? And guilt about gambling and what-not and everything else... and erm...'

Something about his response had felt simultaneously rehearsed and rushed, as if these words of explanation were losing their power and authenticity. It felt like my words had somehow bounced off him and ricocheted back to me. His voice was often lilting and nostalgic when he spoke, which I had become used to – a kind of lyrical retelling of his life story to make sense of the present. However, this felt different. I experienced these words as tumbling, searching blindly for an explanation rather than the felt-sense of 'why' that I had been wondering about. At the time I had an emerging sense that I could try to forge a communion with a deeper part of Bobby.

'It feels like you can't risk feeling like you're a good person.'

Bobby paused here and thought a while, his voice and gaze lowered.

'I'd rather feel being a bad person than being a good person.'

Over our time together, in his story-telling, Bobby reconstructed with me a life of pain, hardship and regret. Born into poverty in Falkirk to a resourceful but overbearing 'monster' of a mother and a distant, unloving father who was in and out of casual work, Bobby recalled them not having enough money for shoes when he was a small boy. His father died when he was young and his mother, a frequent gambler, remarried and, he suspected, began selling what few possessions they had to fund her habit. He was the youngest of five boys and one of his strongest memories of his early years was walking for miles to take money to the local bookies for one of his family and (remembered with considerable shame) carrying notes from his mother to one of her lovers.

Bobby told me he was hard of hearing even as a child, but this was never formally diagnosed during his school years. He became isolated at school, inevitably acted out and was sent to the back of the class for poor behaviour, which exacerbated his inability to hear the lessons. At home he was frequently told he was stupid and was knocked about by his siblings – something he told me was regarded as normal. But Bobby was resourceful, charming and funny, even at that age, and on his frequent visits to the butchers, sent by his mother, he enquired about a Saturday job, which he was duly offered. 'Butchers was a good trade in those days,' he told me. He left school to apprentice proudly as a butcher and worked there until he was 16. He recounted, sadly, that this was the first environment within which he felt accepted.

At 16 he lost his job dramatically after an argument with his boss. He described having some kind of a breakdown at this time and was sent by his family to a mental hospital, one of the largest in Scotland. He knew he was treated with ECT, but the rest of his memories of this period were hazy. None of his family visited him in the two years he was there. Notably, he still thought of this as one of the times in his life when he felt truly cared for.

When he left hospital he met Mary, who was 16 at the time. She quickly became pregnant out of wedlock and, as this was considered to be shameful then, was taken by her family down to south-east England to see out the pregnancy with a distant relative. The baby was subsequently adopted. Bobby remembers being torn about what to do, feeling that he had let Mary down and had not done the right thing. He eventually followed Mary to where she lived, courted her again, married her and settled there. He apprenticed as a builder and they established a modest life together. They had four more children and eventually found and rebuilt a relationship with the child they had given up for adoption.

Bobby told me he had very few friends, worked as hard as he could and liked nothing more than to come home to Mary at the end of the working day. She kept house and kept the family going. But, to let off steam, Bobby began to gamble. He told me that this became quite a habit and he wasted a lot of his earnings on it. Mary deserved more, he said; she never complained, but he gave her and the kids very little of his attention, affection or, in the end, money. 'I wasn't one for talking, or saying "I love you",' he told me; 'I was very difficult to live with. They deserved better.'

Listening back to the recordings now, and even in the moment, within the session, the fumbling words he used earlier to explain why he was a bad man are a little out of character. This was a man who had been able, usually, to explain and reflect on moments in his life with huge alacrity.

'I'd rather feel being a bad person than being a good person.'

In the recording, my voice here is quiet and gentle. I felt like we were close to something, but I had no idea what.

'Do you have a sense of why?'

'I don't know.' He paused, and we sat in silence for a considerable while.

It is true that, throughout the narrative about his life, Bobby had persistently presented himself as bad and undeserving of love. This appeared to be the 'I' he had constructed through generalising his interactions with others across his life, from his mother who was encumbered with yet another young child, his siblings who taunted him, his school teachers who didn't understand him and a boss who rejected him. Viewed from an existential perspective, I conceptualised it as a sedimented belief, laid down like layers of rock, that had served him well but was now holding him back. I was frustrated with the story, as it was so incongruent with how I experienced him. Challenging fundamental beliefs with clients can often feel difficult as it can cause them to come into conflict with their very ontology (Spinelli, 2007). How would it be to experience a shift in one's sense of self at the age of 79?

Developmental theory would say that reflection is essential to the task of ageing (Erikson & Erikson, 1997). But what if the narrative of someone's life can be so altered that well-worn pathways of meaning can no longer be followed? When I was training, one of my tutors used to tell us that a counsellor's role is to find a way to tell someone something they don't want to hear in a way that they can hear it. This feels like quite a responsibility but perhaps offers the possibility for transformative change. Bobby had said to me decisively that he preferred to think of himself as bad. I felt in these moments that, by revealing and questioning this strongly held belief, we might unlock the meaning for Bobby of holding onto it and perhaps form a new narrative for him.

And so we sat in silence a while. The way we were positioned in Bobby's cluttered lounge meant he looked out of the patio door while I was facing him. His flat cap, which he always removed as we sat down, was on the arm of the chair and he fiddled with it absent-mindedly, seemingly lost in thought.

'... I don't know,' he said again.

Then, eventually, looking down at the cap, he said: 'For my sins... put it that way.'

These words were heavier, lower in resonance and seemed to come from his core. The word 'sin' had a biblical feel and I sensed it wasn't his word; it felt punitive, like a label. I repeated it, mirroring his tone because I wanted him to know I'd heard it in all its qualities and I wanted our experience of it to stay with us and to confirm I had understood it.

'For your sins.'

'Yes.'

Quietly and slowly now, I said: 'Let me say this and see how it sounds. The things you've done in the past that you're not proud of are so powerful to you that you can't... they stop you from feeling any parts of you that are good.'

'Yeah.'

'Does that...?' I again wanted to check I had grasped it correctly.

'Yeah', he said again, then continued: 'No, it doesn't mean... no, it's – erm [he paused to think]. I remember going to my stepfather's funeral... I didn't, not his funeral... I went to see him, he was dead, and you know, you go up and see them in the coffin, and, erm, there was people about that wanted to comfort me, but I didn't want nothing to do with them, you know, I sort of bolted away.'

'How old were you then?'

'Oh, it was quite late in life, you know. I was quite old, but the same thing happened with my sister. She died in hospital – um, she'd had a terrible, terrible hard time of it, you know, and, erm, when she died, you know, I sort of – uh – got up and rushed out of the room when somebody came with comfort.'

What Bobby had shown me at the very start of this extract was what it was like for him when another person offered comforting or encouraging words that spoke to a part of him that was worthy; he didn't like it. He was now telling me about how, in key moments in his life, when others offered him kindness, his instinct was to run away. The philosopher Martin Buber suggests that, as we are always in constant, ordinary dialogue with each other, all we need to do is notice what is happening and respond in a way that confirms each other as a 'Thou', not an 'It' (Alexander & Goldenberg, 2002). All I had done was to notice the incongruity of the strength and energy with which Bobby held on to his 'I am a bad person' narrative, combined with a felt sense of heavy sadness and resignation when he told me he had sinned and didn't deserve comfort. Perls (1981) believed that neurosis is the result of a discrepancy between verbal awareness and embodied sense of self, and I remember feeling that some part of Bobby wanted to allow this inner part of himself to speak up.

Listening again to the recording of the session, I wonder about my persistence in pursuing this. I notice how hard I seemed to be working. I think I had an innate sense of something more and felt impatient – we were running out of time. One of the realities of working in an agency or organisation in a supportive role is that counselling can often only be offered on a time-limited basis. Bobby had been referred to me from the bereavement support service where I volunteered, which offered only six sessions to clients. Bobby and I had already had more than six sessions, as I had been able to secure an extension to a further six, but I knew we would soon have to work towards an ending. My internal supervisor reflected that we had built up a strong therapeutic alliance that could withstand a little push into the unknown; that I wasn't wading in uninvited – we were going in there together.

Laing states that we should seek to understand clients from a profoundly human place to find the original self and nurse it back to life (1960). What I have noticed when working with clients over the age of 80 is that sometimes the true, inner self can be harder to find, especially if it has been buried through adverse experiences nearly a lifetime ago. Had we taken Bobby's narrative at face value at this point, had I viewed the development of self as pointless for someone in poor health whose view of the world, in his own words, was slowly contracting, who himself told me he was 'not long for this world', what might have happened? The humanistic tradition within which I developed as a counsellor views everyone as having potential for growth and that this growth is enabled through inter-relatedness with others. Philosophically, I subscribe to the notion that our existence is dynamic, always passing through what has been and what has not yet been (Heidegger, cited in van Deurzen, 2002). I have been privileged to work with clients who, despite being towards the end of their lives, don't believe they shouldn't change and grow and, frankly, why should they?

Back in our session, Bobby continued: 'No, I'm just saying that because I don't know what makes me do that. I couldn't be comforted by anybody.'

'No… What does comfort mean?' I wanted to know the particular meaning for him instead of thinking of 'comfort' through my frame of reference. Bobby and I were born 38 years apart, in different countries and into different economic and personal circumstances. I might put a different meaning on the word 'comfort', around which these moments were pivoting, and I wanted to make sure I was with his meaning, not mine. I find language and the particularities of language so important, and particularly when working with difference with clients, whether across language, cultural, racial or age divides.

Bobby said: 'Well, you know, a hug and "How are you?" and "Are you all right?"'

'Ah,' I agreed.

'… I couldn't do that,' he said.

I found myself confused a little by this, as his language – to me at least – seemed muddled, so I said: 'You can't do it? Or you can't have it shown?'

'No, I can't physically… No, I can comfort somebody else, yes,' and he smiled and laughed and the intensity of the moments we were sharing was momentarily broken, 'but I can't be comforted.'

'So, when it's about you,' I clarified.

'Yeah,' and he paused.

'What is it about you that means you can't feel –'

'I don't know,' he interjected quickly.

'– feel,' I continued, 'someone's compassion towards you?'

'I don't know,' and again he paused and looked at the hat before continuing: 'Well, I suppose it's, um, I feel I don't deserve it.'

As had become usual in our sessions, Bobby then spontaneously moved on from this into a lively and descriptive account of his life. Most often than not, it focused on his early years, and today was no exception. Some of what he told me I had heard before but each time brought something new: new meaning or a new detail. Cumulatively and circularly, we seemed to be getting closer to things that held meaning for the life he lived now, but sometimes it also felt like a wild goose chase. His lilting, heavily accented voice was always inviting and what was often being asked of me was to bear witness, but I consciously tried to listen between the words to the story that perhaps wasn't explicitly being told.

For me, one of the most powerful ways of listening to long narrative is to use the whole of my body. I try to notice how I hold my body, its posture and any feelings that I register. I also look for clues or changes in the posture, movement or expressions of the person I am with. Holding onto Gestalt principles, I try to offer this back to them, in case it unlocks meaning or brings more awareness (Clarkson, 1989). When Bobby had been talking earlier about being comforted, he had used his hands to mimic pushing someone away. I repeated the gesture, saying 'You want that away,' and he'd repeated the gesture again and said, 'Nah, keep away from me,' and there was a look of disgust that seemed to take us closer to the emotion of how he responded to comfort.

Now, as Bobby's story developed, I could see his body was tensing. He took me back to age five – he specifically mentioned his age – and how he was rejected at school, and throughout his life consequently, for being stupid. I felt that my presence at this time was merely a background for Bobby to relive past events and make sense of them as he spoke. Rogers (1961/2004) and Maslow (1968), important influencers of the person-centred approach to therapy, believe humans to be inherently growth-orientated, and they challenge counsellors to allow clients to speak freely and to sense for themselves where their areas for growth are. However, I resonate more with the notion that direction towards growth is co-created within the relationship between two people.

Bobby went on to tell me how, from five years old onwards, he was repeatedly punished and it stuck with him. As he told me this, his hand made a fist and he punctuated what he was saying by banging repeatedly on the arm of the chair with each word. I remember that we both looked at his hand as it fell for the last time and laid still, clenched into a fist.

'And I always thought, you know, if somebody's... if somebody's coming to comfort you [pause] they're either looking for something... [pause] or there's something wrong about it.'

We were both silent. Then I responded: 'There's something wrong about somebody comforting you.'

Bobby didn't register my statement but continued: 'And I think I've just touched the situation that happened in my life... that makes me feel like that.' His voice was now quiet, low.

'Yeah,' I said, with the same low resonance, trying to hold us there and let him know I had heard the importance of this.

Louder now, Bobby carried on: 'I've found a point in my head' – here he pointed emphatically to the centre of his head with a straight finger – 'that makes me very wary of people saying anything like you did. Like I said about my mother, I'm going with messages to her fancy man and I liked my stepfather because he was good to me but at the same time I'm betraying him and I'm having to keep it to myself, and it does things with your head, really, you know you don't know whether you're coming or going or where you are.'

Again, the story came out energetically and fast but what I heard within the words was shame. I also felt a sudden jump out of the slow, feeling, embodied place in which we had just been into a cognitive place, into his head, where he had been pointing. Perhaps it wasn't accidental; it felt like a protective mechanism. I responded with a clumsy question, from a thinking rather than a feeling place: 'So this point that you talked about in your head, can you share it?'

In retrospect, this was in the service of my curiosity, rather than for Bobby. Among all the uncertainty, unpredictability and humanness of counselling sessions, there is no undo button; sometimes we simply get things wrong and we can't go back. My response was heavy handed, intrusive even. I remember the tone of his response; the first 'no' sounding hesitant and the second 'no' a gentle, insistent request for privacy that revealed a momentum of something else. I experienced it as a signal of autonomy and self-possession. I remember that my instinctive response welled up from within me involuntarily: 'No, that's private.' I felt that it communicated much more than those three words. I hope I answered from the whole of me, that what Bobby heard was, 'I hear you, I respect you, this is important and I'm sorry.' Perhaps I'm being nostalgic but I feel that, by Bobby knowing and holding his boundaries and by my demonstrating that I thought I heard all that was not said, we both shifted the relationship forward.

It is an occupational hazard of working with older people with many layers of life experience that much of the time is spent focusing on the past. I feel that counselling can be a place for those who are elderly to reflect on the impact of the past within the present – to move from reminiscing and reflecting into meaning-making and growth. These moments with Bobby put in me in mind of what developmental psychiatrist and theorist Daniel Stern (1998) called 'kairos'. This is a moment so laden with potential importance that it pulls people fully into the present. Perhaps due to the focus on historical events in his story-telling, I felt Bobby and I were often distanced from each other. One way of bringing our experience together, I found, was to notice and mirror his gestures. I hoped this would bring me back to him and bring him to his body and emotion. The philosopher Merleau-Ponty (1945) maintained that we don't *have* a body, we *are* a body, so that bodily movement is emotion itself. It feels natural to me that this informs the therapeutic encounter, as it does in Gestalt (Perls, 1969) and focusing (Madison, 2014), among others. So, in this encounter with Bobby, each time we made connection with the body, we were able to move forward and closer to emotional connections.

As I write these reflections, I find myself moving towards something of a denouement and, in some ways, wishing there wasn't one. In and of itself, this part of our work together was therapeutic and transforming for both of us. Much of what happened was subtle movement within the intersubjective space – two human beings fumbling through an experience of words, movement and all of our senses. We moved through narrative into meaning and, to a certain extent, identified something that was holding Bobby back from processing his grief. One of our contemporary grief theorists, Robert Neimeyer (2005), proposes that the distress of grief can be reduced when meaning is explored and assimilated into the bereaved's life story. He calls on us to promote a narrative, creative approach to finding meaning in loss so that the bereaved person may move forward in life with an identity that has evolved through the grief. So, if finding comfort was not possible for Bobby, how could he find any acceptance of or feel at peace with the loss of his beloved Mary?

Bobby continued, almost as if I wasn't there: 'No, but it's helping me, no I can't… um… but I can see why, why, it's such, such a relief… because I…' and he held his hand to his chest and exhaled.

I exhaled with him.

'… it's like opening a door,' and here he pivoted his arm from the elbow to mimic a door opening.

I repeated the gesture: 'So it's like this.'

'Yes, it's like almost like opening myself up to be able to be comforted.'

'That's amazing.'

Bobby looked straight at me now: 'Yes, it is amazing because it's… you know, you look for things that cause you to behave in such a way and I think that's, that's what it was.'

'And you did this.' I touched my hand to my chest. 'You held your hand to your chest and you said, "It's a relief".' Bobby had moved into the third person just now and I was trying to bring it back to him.

'Yes.'

'How does it feel in your body when you say that?'

'It feels as if I've got rid of a great weight off my shoulders…'

'You feel lighter.'

'… because, put it this way, I probably blame myself, but it wasn't me at all.'

'No… and you can see that now.'

Bobby nodded at me.

'We should take a moment just to acknowledge that that's happened. That sounds like a very profound realisation for you.'

There was a long pause. Then Bobby replied: 'Yes, it is,' and exhaled slowly.

'And I notice you're taking a breath.' I mirrored his breath.

We sat in silence for a little while. I remember it was long enough for me to notice the carriage clock ticking.

Then Bobby said: 'I think someone did something very bad to me when I was about five years of age; that's what it's about. And I thought it was my fault. And most of my life has been directed by that.'

Spinelli (2007) argues that our problems are at the nexus between us and the world and that we don't solve them, we live them. Bobby showed me right at the start of this encounter that he couldn't tolerate compassionate things being said about him, which enabled us, together, to meet with and explore the part of himself that felt shameful and rejected. We did this as much through movement and gesture as through words. We were able to offer the possibility of something new happening by using the microcosm of our relationship to become a catalyst for self-reflection and a rewriting of Bobby's story (Bott & Howard, 2012). At the age of five, something bad had happened, which he internalised as being his fault. Much of how he had lived his life had been informed by a sense of shame and rejection. He had told me in one of our earlier sessions that he had never loved anyone in his whole life. It is one of the moments I remember most strongly from all my clinical work to date. I recall feeling physically empty inside; I remember the sensation being so strong and the fear that I felt being so overwhelming that I wanted to run out of the house. Later in the session described here, Bobby reminded me of this; he said that the caring part of him that could accept love was buried deep inside and the barriers were very high, but he felt it would be possible to release it.

'It's all there, isn't it. I feel different now. I think I can say that I don't hate myself anymore, that I might be able to be more of a whole person.'

As I'm writing this, I am diligently listening back to the account, trying to catch any inconsistency and make sure that I reflect what happened as accurately as I can. I realise it sounds too good to be true. I genuinely offer this account of Bobby not to demonstrate my capability as a counsellor but rather to celebrate the power and possibility of being with another person who is attuned to what is happening in the room and does nothing other than witness, notice and journey alongside another. I also offer it as an antidote to Freud's assertion that therapy over the age of 65 is not worthwhile (Bollas, 2007); as testament to the potential of humans to find growth, and as a challenge to our health and social policy-makers who have yet to realise the value and worth in investing in the emotional wellbeing of older people.

References

Alexander Z, Goldenberg H (2002). Between persons: the narrow ridge where I and Thou meet. In: du Plock S (ed). *Further Existential Challenges to the Psychotherapeutic Theory and Practice: papers from Existential Analysis*. London: Society for Existential Practice (pp154–165).

Bollas C (2007). *The Freudian Moment*. London: Karnac Books.

Bott D, Howard P (2012). *The Therapeutic Encounter: a cross-modality approach*. London: Sage Publications.

Clarkson P (1989). *Gestalt Counselling in Action*. London: Sage Publications.

Erikson JM, Erikson EH (1997). *The Life Cycle Completed: a review*. New York, NY: WW Norton & Company.

Laing RD (1960). *The Divided Self: an existential study in sanity and madness*. London: Tavistock Publications.

Lewis CS (1952/2012). *Mere Christianity*. London: William Collins.

Madison G (ed) (2014). *Theory and Practice of Focusing-Oriented Psychotherapy: beyond the talking cure*. London: Jessica Kingsley Publishers.

Maslow AH (1968). *Toward a Psychology of Being* (2nd ed). New York, NY: Van Nostrand Reinhold.

Mearns D, Cooper M (2005). *Working at Relational Depth in Counselling and Psychotherapy*. London: Sage Publications.

Merleau-Ponty M (2002). *Phenomenology of Perception* (C Smith trans). London: Routledge Classics.

Neimeyer RA (2005). Grief, loss, and the quest for meaning. *Bereavement Care* 24(2): 27–30.

Perls FS (1969). *Gestalt Therapy Verbatim*. Gouldsboro, ME: The Gestalt Journal Press.

Phillips SB (2011). Up close and personal: a consideration of the role of personal therapy in the development of a psychotherapist. In: Klein RH, Bernard HS, Schermer VL (eds). *On Becoming a Psychotherapist: the personal and professional journey*. Oxford: Oxford University Press (pp144–164).

Plato (c369BC/2014). *Theaetetus* (J McDowell trans). Oxford: Oxford University Press.

Rogers CR (1961/2004). *On Becoming a Person: a therapist's view of psychotherapy*. London: Constable & Robinson.

Sartre J-P (1938/2000). *Nausea*. London: Penguin Classics.

Slater R (1995). *The Psychology of Growing Old: looking forward*. Buckingham: Open University Press.

Spinelli E (2002). *The Mirror and the Hammer: challenging orthodoxies in therapeutic thought*. London: Sage Publications.

Spinelli E (2007). *Practising Existential Therapy: the relational world*. London: Sage Publications.

Stern DN (1998). The process of therapeutic change involving implicit knowledge: some implications of developmental observations for adult psychotherapy. *Infant Mental Health Journal* 19(3): 300–308.

Tornstam L (1997). Gerotranscendence: the contemplative dimension of aging. *Journal of Aging Studies* 11(2): 143–154.

Van Deurzen E (2002). Heidegger's challenge of authenticity. In: du Plock S (ed). *Further Existential Challenges to the Psychotherapeutic Theory and Practice: papers from Existential Analysis*. London: Society for Existential Practice (pp370–379).

Viney L (1993). *Life Stories: personal construct therapy with the elderly*. Chichester: Wiley.

Keeping up appearances
Joan

'All that is gold does not glitter,
Not all those who wander are lost;
The old that is strong does not wither,
Deep roots are not reached by the frost.'
JRR Tolkien, *The Lord of the Rings*

Joan was referred to me by a physiotherapist. Nine months before, she had suffered a stroke, and she was now recovering independently at home. Since she was unable to drive, our sessions took place at her home.

Working with clients in their home environment is a rich experience, offering the opportunity to establish meaning, reminisce and evoke emotional responses from the everyday objects that surround the client. However, it also offers the possibility of seduction into a set of assumptions and a frame of reference that can be held subconsciously by the therapist. It can lull the visiting therapist into a role of 'helper' or 'visitor', causing us to slip, unaware, into a less phenomenological way of being. I felt both responses triggered in my work with Joan, and I found that, in my reflections and supervision throughout our work together, I had to hold steady to my course as an existential counsellor and to resist the call to be like all the other helping individuals that surrounded her.

I'm not exaggerating when I say that arriving at Joan's house for our first session was like the opening pages of a cosy novel. To find the house, you had to turn down an unadopted lane, with greenery flanking it on either side. Narrow, almost hidden gateways led off it to houses obscured from view by foliage. It was almost midsummer and, even in the middle of the day, there was a cool darkness in the lane as I parked the car near to the wooden gate bearing the house name and stepped out onto the gravel. The house was approached via an extensive, colourful and clearly lovingly designed garden. To navigate to the door, I first stepped through a cast-iron archway trailing flowers, then round past a wooden summer house with jaunty gingham curtains. The house was a low, stone cottage, its doorway surrounded by a stone and slate porch, in the lee of which were a garden seat and a boot jack.

Who could not arrive at that place without having gained some sense of the person inside and the life they might live? Even as I write this, I notice I am checking back through the prose for embellishment, misremembered elements or romantic fantasy, and there are none. The lane, the garden, the archway, the house and the porch are exactly as they were. But what a picture they created in my mind as I waited for the door to open.

I believe supervision to be a powerful tool for actively and supportively opening blind spots, whether culturally created or constructed by our own personal experiences. I find these moments in supervision when the fog clears to be like the final phase of the Gestalt cycle, where the impasse is resolved (Clarkson, 1989). Once, with another client, I was completely stuck, unable to reach her and establish a deep, reciprocal therapeutic relationship. When I took this impasse to my supervisor, she asked if I could see any similarities with other people I had met before. She sensed from the level of frustration and 'stuckness' I was describing that this client wasn't unique in my awareness, that some patterned response had kicked in. She also used her felt sense, her whole body, to notice my frown, my clenched hands and my muddled language. Suddenly all became clear: 'She's my English teacher from secondary school!'

These experiences in supervision have given birth to a keen internal supervisor within me, who hears and sees with different ears and extra eyes what I might not be seeing. Working across a considerable age gap – often 40 years or more – I always try to orientate myself to the unique cultural, social and relational experiences of the person before me, rather than let myself be pulled into cliché or draw impulsively on personal experiences (Birren et al, 1991). Therefore, I found myself at the door of Joan's house with open eyes and ears, acutely conscious of the narrative I was constructing without having even met her yet.

Our first couple of sessions covered a lot of the details of Joan's life and what brought her to counselling – factually at least, if not yet emotionally, but we will get to that. During our sessions, Joan sat in an armchair under the casement window of her cosy lounge. Our sessions were in the mid-afternoon and we met weekly for six months, during which time the seasons changed, but usually we had the afternoon light on us in an otherwise dark room. From the chair, Joan could see out into her well-tended garden, where she loved to spend her time when she was able. Always perfectly made up, wearing neat, bright clothes and coordinated earrings, she spoke with a barely discernible northern accent and a slight slur that betrayed the stroke that she had suffered the year before. Next to her, on a small side table, were her phone, a pad and pen (invariably with a list in progress), cards and letters that were pertinent, and her diary. Here was a lady in charge of her life: capable, strong, coping.

Her unfolding story was of a practical, independent, socially involved individual who had progressed through a relatively unremarkable but meaningful and rewarding life. She was born in Newcastle, the only child of hard-working parents running their own butcher's shop. She took herself to and from school and youth club with little practical involvement from her parents. Although she did feel loved by them, they were not around her for many hours of the day. She grew into an independent, forthright young woman and took herself off to retail college, reporting to me that her parents weren't there to say goodbye or take her to the station. Once she'd left home, she rarely returned, and she moved to the south of England and found a series of jobs in retail management. She met and married John, a schoolmaster, and gave up work once their children were born. John had died about two years before we met, but she had reconstructed her social life and had, up until her stroke, continued with the varied social and community activities in which she had been involved – not least, as chair of the local Women's Institute.

Joan and John had two children, a boy and a girl, and gradually built a relatively comfortable life of work, golfing, Women's Institute and children, with the occasional holiday by the coast. Their eldest, Diana, married a lawyer, and gave them three grandchildren. When the grandchildren were still all under the age of 12, Diana was diagnosed with cancer, which progressed very quickly, and she died at the age of 40.

As Joan was talking me about Diana, her voice and her demeanour were unchanged. I remember trying to stay very still, in an attempt to feel into the nuances of her lived experience of telling me about her daughter's death, 20 years ago. I could feel nothing; I noticed no change. I kept quiet to allow us to pause. Joan looked at me in a matter-of-fact way.

'How is it to talk about Diana?' I wondered out loud.

'It's fine.'

I paused again.

'Oh well, it was hard at the time, but you just sort of get on with it don't you,' she elaborated.

'You just "get on with it",' I reflected.

Joan shrugged: 'Well, what else is there to do?' – this said with the faintest hint of irritation.

I kept the space open and, after a longer pause, Joan sighed: 'My husband didn't like big displays of emotion. We never used to really talk about Diana's death. He was a practical man. Sometimes I would go upstairs and have a cry from time to time, but yes, I just kind of got on with it. Her children needed me too. I was concerned for them and they didn't need me to fall apart at that time.'

'And now?'

'Well, what's the use in bringing all that up now?'

Not for the first or last time, I felt that Joan's emotions were being tidied away.

In that moment, what felt right was to show her that her displays of emotion were welcome with me – to offer her some space to express her feelings of loss. I wish I could say that, when I offered it, Joan was able to do this, and to cry all the tears she had held back for all those 20 years, but this isn't a sentimental novel and humans are not that biddable. This was our second session and our relationship was still developing. The practical part of Joan was persistent; it would take time, patience and encouragement to find and nurture the other parts.

As babies, we look for clues as to how to respond to an experience by noticing how the other person responds (Stern, 1985). As we grow up, it is this same pattern that drives us to internalise others' reactions and turn them into our 'conditions of worth' (Rogers, 1951/2003) that themselves drive our beliefs, behaviours and actions. As new-borns we are expelled, vulnerable and unfinished, into the world and we come to find ourselves through interaction with our families and society (Bott & Howard, 2012). From an existential perspective, these are sedimented beliefs, established early on, and they form the foundation of our ontology (Mearns & Cooper, 2005; Spinelli 2007). Having them challenged is understandably difficult for the client, as it is for the counsellor to challenge them.

When working with older adults, these sedimented ways of being can feel even harder to challenge – they have been of service for many decades. I often see my job as a counsellor, with elderly clients or otherwise, to be forensically focused on both the whole picture, the selfhood of the person I am with, and on the minutiae of our intersubjective communication and my felt sense of them in the room. I actively look for inconsistency and bring it into our awareness. It was this stance that eventually moved us forward, a little.

We had been exploring the difficulties of socialising without her husband, as many of her friends went on holiday or outings as couples. We were talking more generally about friendships when Joan adjusted her gaze very slightly and looked down towards her hands:

'…and as you know, unfortunately I was an only child…' A pause.

'Why "unfortunately"?' I asked.

'What do you mean?'

'You said "unfortunately", and I wondered what that meant for you.'

'Oh, I see. Well, you know, people who have no siblings find it harder to make friends and have to be quite solitary.'

'But we are not talking about "people", we are talking about you,' I replied gently, in a low voice and with an encouraging smile. Often, Joan would move into the third person or make generalisations when we got close to something important. This was a pattern we had already noticed so I was reminding her of this.

'Well, I had no one at home to talk to. My parents worked long hours and I had no siblings to rub along with. I just kind of got on with things.'

'You wanted things to be different.'

'No, I don't remember feeling that; I just didn't want to bother Mum and Dad with stuff as they had enough on their plate with the business.'

This small moment within one of our many sessions opened the door for us to explore how, over the years, this early experience was perpetuated in her long (happy) marriage to John, who wasn't keen on big emotions, and how it meant that many of her strong feelings and experiences of grief, sadness and anger had not been outwardly expressed.

As an aside, and here I am conscious of the danger of generalising, Joan was eight years old when World War Two ended; she lived her early childhood in a state of war. I was broadly aware of Bronfenbrenner's theory of chronosystemic influence (1993): of the relationship of time and place to a person and their influence on their sense of self. It is not something I have studied in depth, but I have explored it from time to time when it has emerged in the counselling room. At the same time, I try to hold myself to account for any assumptions I might make based on my tacit understanding of what life might have been like for people growing up at that time.

Anecdotally, clients I have worked with, and my own grandparents, have recounted how most families experienced at least one loss during the war, if not more. It became something so ordinary that it was no longer talked about. For the fathers of that generation, returning from the war and re-assimilating into everyday life was hard, and even harder if the horrors they had experienced were not talked about. For the mothers, adjusting to their husband's return was hard too. Here were fathers too traumatised to talk about what they had been through and whose mantra, perhaps, was to get on with the business of living and not dwell on the past.

All of this is within our shared cultural narrative, but it doesn't have to be the particular narrative of the person I am with in the room. However, with this generation, it often seems to hinder the process of forming an open, trusting therapeutic alliance. I find it requires persistence and patience on my part to model the therapeutic process and create an environment where feelings, emotions and felt sense can be explored.

This was something I experienced in my work with Joan. As part of the contracting process, I try to check out the expectations of counselling with the clients I work with. In her paper exploring working with difference in supervision, Hilde Rapp (2000) recommends that counsellors explore their clients' culturally-constructed expectations of what counselling is, so that there is an open dialogue about what is happening. Joan was feeling low after returning home from hospital following the stroke; she was coping with both her reduced mobility and her increased dependency without her husband. As is usual, at the end of our first session I had checked in with her on how we were doing, and she seemed to be happy for me to come back and comfortable with what she had experienced.

A few times in the initial sessions, she had asked me for my opinion or advice and, as I always do, I responded by bringing it back to what she felt was right. However, after a month or so, Joan began the session very abruptly by saying that she wasn't sure if we were getting anywhere. She had discussed it with her physiotherapist and she felt she needed more advice and guidance on how to cope with the issues we had been exploring, like lack of sleep and trying to relax when her mobility wasn't so good. My initial response was a contraction of irritation in my abdomen and a real sense of not being good enough. I registered this feeling and allowed it to resonate within me while I reflected her frustration back to her. I went back over what we had been exploring in the sessions and repeated what I had told her: that I worked from a belief that, by exploring and nurturing all parts of her, she would find the answers within herself. 'Yes, yes, I get all that, but sometimes I just need you to tell me what to do,' she replied irritably. I replied, honestly, that I now felt under considerable pressure to do this.

Reflecting on this many months later, I am struck by the many layers of experiencing and influence that can happen within one tiny intersubjective moment, like this one. There are times in my work when I am conscious of my own patterned reactions being triggered and this was one of them. The perfectionist in me was activated at this point: the part that doesn't like to fail – the youngest sibling with something to prove, the daughter of a hardworking, ambitious, loving father with all her best interests at heart; the bright student apparently breezing through academic success but concealing the hours of graft, discipline and worry. This part of me heard this feedback and wanted to wade in with a solution that would satisfy Joan, to work as hard as she was asking me to.

My instinct as a humanistic, existential therapist is to work phenomenologically with what is happening between me and the client, as it is happening. Theoretically, this felt like a moment of rupture with potential for repair and maybe for growth – a mirror of the early development phase of negotiating the realities of psychic differentiation from our caregivers to find our own, sure footing (Stern, 1985). The practitioner in me welcomed this opportunity to work with what was happening and perhaps deepen our therapeutic relationship. I knew I was one of a number of people who came to Joan's house to help her in various ways: she had a cleaner, a carer who came twice a week to make her breakfast and do some light housework, a physiotherapist and the person who delivered her prescription drugs. I have noticed when visiting those who are infirm that counselling can be grouped with the category of 'people who help me' and wondered if this might be what was happening here. It felt like a good place to start.

'You would like me to tell you what to do?'

'Yes, because I am really struggling these past few weeks and I just really need some help. I am finding sleep difficult and I feel very stressed and down. I find it really helpful when people, like Carol, give me guidance on what will work.'

Carol was the physiotherapist who had recommended me to Joan. She had called me and said that Joan was quite attached to her coming each week and reluctant to end their work, even though she was nearly ready to, from a physical point of view. They'd discussed some counselling as a way of dealing with her low mood and frustration. Reflecting on this now, I could see that Joan's expectations of therapy had been set up in this very first, indirect interaction: Joan needed some additional 'help' that the physio wasn't equipped to provide.

'Joan, I now feel that I have to give you some advice, but what I would like to suggest instead is that we explore these feelings you have talked about and what it is that makes you feel you need my help.'

I remember feeling pulled powerfully between these two instincts – professional and personal – that I've mentioned. I also felt the pull to actively help and wanted to resist that and see if together we could create a different outcome that might ripple out into other parts of Joan's life. All that I had learned about Joan's past life told me she was an independent person who knew her own mind and was eminently capable. I believe that, even if all we do as counsellors is notice the patterns we and our client are being pulled into, there is still the potential for something different and new to happen (Bott & Howard, 2012).

As the session progressed from here, we began to talk about the impasse that Joan experienced when things went wrong or didn't progress as she was hoping. Her right arm and right leg were affected by her stroke. She was able to walk, albeit a little slower than before, but the mobility in her arm and dexterity in her fingers had become her barometer for how well she was rehabilitating. Often, during our sessions, she would show me how well or badly it was going that week. Raising her arm close to shoulder level would elicit a proud smile, but if she couldn't straighten out her stiff fingers, a dark frown would appear. On a day or a week of increased stiffness, Joan would feel despondent, do fewer of her exercises and venture out less, which increased her feelings of despair. 'You kind of feel it's not worth it, what's the point?' she said. She went on to say that it was in these darker moments that she felt more keenly the lack of family support around her.

Joan's family were dispersed: her son and grandson lived two hours away by car; her grown-up grandchildren on her daughter's side lived far away or abroad and she was not in close contact with her son-in-law. I had nodded in understanding when she mentioned lack of family support but, realising now that I had drawn my own conclusions, I wanted to check I had understood her meaning.

'Are you saying that you wish your family lived nearer, that they visited more, making the harder times easier?'

'No, not really. They do what they can. It is just so unfair that I am, at this time of my life, going through this, and this is exactly when I need my daughter, but I don't have her.' Her voice emphasised each of the last five words.

We paused, Joan was looking down at the floor. For a while we sat in silence. This felt vital to what had been going on in this session.

Eventually Joan looked up at me: 'Mmmmmm,' she said with pursed lips.

'Oh well,' she said, and sighed.

Much of what she had told me about her daughter, Diana, had been a narrative of regret and loss that became less raw over the course of our sessions together, but now we had arrived at a new meaning. Living out old age now, without her life partner, with a son who was practical at best, distant at worst, had brought Diana's death into stark relief for Joan. This was the time in her life when she should have been enjoying the changing of roles, receiving the support of her emotionally literate, caring and creative daughter. Perhaps the invitation to me had been to fulfil some of that role, alongside the several other women, curiously also all in their 40s, who supported her each week.

The counselling relationship is a dance between two people and, as with dancing, sometimes the bodies move together as though by instinct, imperceptibly, to create a new position, rather than follow explicit, discernible steps. I believe there are moments in a counselling relationship where two people arrive at something together and move through the moment, knowing what has happened but without it having to be talked about. This felt like a silent, authentic moment of meeting (Stern, 1998), where the intersubjective context between us shifted in a way that caused both of us to feel what was happening, without words. Eventually, after the 'Oh well' and a brief, contemplative silence, we moved on. However, it seemed to me that we had both shifted positions in a way that was meaningful – we had moved from Joan's surface irritation with her physical limitations to honour, at greater depth, the loss she had experienced when her daughter died, which was, in some ways, the loss of a nurturing, feminine influence in her life.

At the end of this session, noticing the iPad on the table in front of us, I asked Joan if she was able to download apps. She said she could. I gave her the name of two mindfulness apps that she might find helpful to calm her and allow her to rest when her sleep was disturbed or she was feeling anxious and frustrated. We also explored what other methods of relaxation or nourishment she ordinarily enjoyed, and Joan immediately said that swimming and taking a bath had helped her in the past. Having a bath independently had been unimaginable in the earlier stages of her rehabilitation, but it was starting to be a possibility now and she had been discussing it with her physiotherapist. When we talked about what was holding her back, she said she lacked confidence that she could do it unaided, so we made a plan together that she would ask her physiotherapist for more practice and guidance to help with this. In essence, I was helping, but not as part of a patterned response on both our parts and hopefully in a way that didn't distract us from the therapeutic journey we were on. Returning to the dance metaphor, I'm sure, if I were able to watch a video of this whole session, it would look clumsy – like two people trying to dance together for the first time and trying not to trip each other up or stand on each other's toes.

During this session, and in many others, Joan voiced her frustration that she had not recovered from her stroke in the ways she had hoped. She felt very much in conflict with her body: that her outward limitations didn't match the determined and capable person within. These moments when Joan's body was not co-operating or she was feeling down had exposed her internal dialogue ('Oh for goodness sake, why won't it just move? It should be better by now!'; 'I just tell myself to pull myself together, there's no point dwelling on things, they will just get me down'). I had noticed that, even with some prompting, Joan struggled to find an alternative internal voice that was nurturing and kind. The voice that was most prominent appeared to be constructed through her early experiences and an adult life that was all about capable doing and sorting – something she readily identified for herself: the busy, hardworking parents necessarily preoccupied with running their business; the practical husband who didn't brook emotions. Remember Joan's side table – the lists, the diary and the letters? I wondered aloud how it would be to try a kinder, softer internal voice. What might it say differently?

These conversations about Joan's harsh, business-like attitude towards herself and her recovery opened, unexpectedly, an exploration of how she had been as a mother, some of which was painful for her to reflect on. Joan told me she felt she had been too distant with her children, not focused enough on their emotional needs. Specifically, she said she hadn't openly told them she loved them (even though she conceded that they would have felt loved by her). Erikson's theory of human development in old age suggests that a necessary task is to reflect upon and accept the inalterability of the past. He mentions that, even though regrets and failures in the past are things that can't be overcome, the process of trying to change them through reflection is an essential and healthy part of the later stages of life (Erikson & Erikson, 1997). I rather prefer the theory of gerotranscendence, which asserts that our selves are circular and that the process of reflecting on painful past experiences helps us redefine our experience in the present (Tornstarm, 1997). Holding this attitude allowed me to encourage Joan to explore her regret while looking for ways to incorporate a shift in herself that might bring about change in her present.

One of the central themes of our work together was how difficult it was for Joan to cope with her enforced solitude, especially now she couldn't drive. Her life before her stroke, which she had reconstructed without apparent difficulty following her husband's death, consisted of walking with friends, swimming and taking tea at the golf club, where she had been a long-standing member, running the local Women's

Institute, playing whist one evening a week with friends, and attending her weekly local 'knit and natter' club. Each of these artefacts of the life before her stroke were in some way denied to her now, depriving her of the natural ebb and flow of social contact and participation. Even just walking up the road in the community in which she had lived for 30 years was now a struggle, an event to be planned for only if the weather were fine and she wasn't too tired.

Loneliness has been widely researched in recent years and has received a great deal of attention both in the media and in health and social policy-making, due to its economic impact. It has been an unexpected consequence of the seemingly laudable shift from institutionalising older people to supporting them to continue to live independently in their own homes. Loneliness is now acknowledged to be the single most important influencer of ill health, physical and mental, in people of all ages. The Royal College of General Practitioners estimated in 2017 that, of the 1.1 million Britons reported to be lonely, 50% were more likely to die prematurely than those with strong social connections (Campbell, 2017). It concluded that loneliness carries as much risk of early death as diabetes.

However, later-life theorists such as Erikson and Erikson (1997) and commentators on ageing, such as Scrutton (1999), often focus on solitude and quietude as offering a space for finding meaning in the life that has been lived. They maintain that lone contemplation frees us from distractions and restrictions and allows us to be creative in our meaning-making. However, they argue, this is only if disengagement in society or community is through choice. In his essay on solitude, Grieder (2002) tells us that solitude can only be existentially significant when chosen with awareness. With Maggie (Chapter 1), this withdrawal into self, into silence and quietness in her final weeks, felt like a gentle and natural process of withdrawal from life. With Joan, it was vastly different. Her enforced solitude was existentially significant. How could we work together to allow her to participate in life again in a way that allowed her true self to flourish?

The key to this was being able to drive. In my counselling practice, I continually try to check my ego. If clients experience growth and change, it needn't be because of our sessions. Nothing is more fascinating and more likely to create a sense of jubilation in me than the session that starts with, 'I'm feeling so much better, you are not going to believe this but...' in relation to a new relationship, a new job, an ended relationship, a hug of a friend or a myriad happenings and changes outside the counselling relationship that have made all the difference and unlocked new possibility for clients. It will often be something unrelated to what happens within the counselling relationship that makes the biggest difference. I always hold in my mind an anecdote told by existential therapist Ernesto Spinelli in a workshop I once attended. He described with great humility and humour a client who started a session by saying how much better he felt. Spinelli asked his client what had been so transformative, to which the client replied that it was a simple hand gesture. Not the power of the therapeutic relationship, not the vibrant philosophical challenge of the existential debate; a hand gesture!

My commitment to those I work with is, at the very least, to provide a reflecting, accepting environment from which they may be able to advance to something new. I believe the way to achieve this is to see beyond the entrapments or frailties of age and find and speak to the true self within. In some ways, this mirrors the concept of the all-important secure base in developmental theory. This asserts that is the close attention of another that allows the young baby to develop a secure sense of self from which they can begin to explore the world (Bowlby, 1969). I find myself wondering at the experience of someone aged 85 or 90 who feels themselves to be overlooked or ignored. This person may be categorised as 'old', so their true self and potential are overlooked by those around them. We see it all too often: medical professionals talking over someone's head to a nurse or a relative; older people being served a cup of tea without first having been asked their preference. The intentions may be good, but the net effect is to render invisible the person who should be at the centre, who then loses confidence and belief in their own ability to take risks and grow.

Joan was hoping to be assessed to see if she could handle an adapted car, despite her reduced mobility. The necessary steps were to have lessons, take a test and then, if successful, apply for her licence and buy a car. This all seemed so far off, but she was determined to try and needed very little encouragement to do so. Our time together each week was often a place to reflect on this process as it unfolded: the excitement of being assessed as fit to have lessons; the trepidation of driving a car for the first time since her stroke; the hope that she would be able to go out and do what she wanted to do; the fear of not passing her test, and her anger and frustration with the lengthy, complicated way that the DVLA operated. Our sessions became a place to explore all this, as well as to experience her exhaustion throughout the process.

However, I noticed over time that, while I was becoming increasingly proud and excited for Joan, she remained relatively matter of fact about her achievements. Her critical, practical inner dialogue, as we explored it, was saying, 'Well, you have got this far but there is so far to go' or 'Don't get your hopes up, it might not happen'. My instincts were to fist pump and hug her as each milestone was reached – quite a contrast. It was hard for her to admit she was gaining ground, or at least it was hard for her to voice that, unbidden. Once more, perhaps slightly clumsily, the opportunity for us to challenge this came out of a moment of discord.

At the same time as she was slowly but steadily progressing towards her driving goal, Joan continued to be niggled by the attitude of others towards her. Trips away were one example. A hallmark of the progress she had made following the death of her husband had been that she had been able to take a trip with their social group, despite being the only person travelling alone. It had taken considerable courage and she had enjoyed it. Now, as I was notifying Joan of an impending week's break at the start of a session, she said: 'I suppose it is half term? Oh, everyone seems to be away that week. Carol is away then too. And over the next few weeks, my friends are all away as it's out of season and, with the milder temperatures, they always seem to go away at this time of year.'

'This frustrates you,' I concurred.

'Well, it's just that I'd like to go away but no one seems to want to go with me.'

'No one wants to take a holiday with you.'

'Well, I haven't asked them but I daren't; they don't even seem comfortable taking me swimming in case something happens to me. They aren't going to want to go away with me, are they.'

'What would it be like to ask them? What is your fear?'

'Oh, that they will say no and I will feel upset, or, worse, they will say yes and then I will feel conscious that they will be worrying about me and not enjoying their holiday.'

'It feels really important for you to go away.'

'Yes, well, it's part of who I was before this happened and I was just getting there after John died and now I am back to square one.'

'Could you go alone?'

'Oh no, it would be too hard.'

Now, I feel I can sometimes be quite emphatic once I get behind something. There are times when I notice this and temper it back into a more exploratory tone, but today that didn't feel right – emphatic I was going to be. As an existentially informed counsellor, I believe in the power of a dynamic interchange with clients (van Deurzen-Smith, 2012), and I also believe that, when something feels inconsistent or out of place, this should be brought into awareness.

'Joan, so far in the last couple of months you have overcome considerable physical limitations and shown incredible bravery and determination. You've not only taken an assessment in a strange car in a place you have never been before, but you've also gone through two-hour driving lessons that have exhausted you and have now passed your test and got your licence back. People half your age may struggle with any one of those. I wonder why you think you can't go on holiday by yourself?'

These are the moments when, as a humanistic, self-subscribed non-directional counsellor, I feel my stomach flip over in fear. Did I go too far here? I believe I may have even held my breath.

'Yes, I have been rather brave I suppose. Do you think I have?'

'I suppose it doesn't matter if I feel you have…'

Quickly and sharply, Joan replied, 'It does matter.'

'Yes, I do. I have so much admiration for how determined and courageous you have been.'

'Well, yes. Then maybe it is something I could think about.'

Once again, I found myself wondering about my role in creating a space where Joan could express insecurity and receive validation and reassurance, despite her apparent strength of character. Had her inherent capability obscured a more vulnerable part who sought support and strength from relationships around her, maybe originally from her husband and daughter, and now from those who formed the helping frame around her life, including me?

In the end, I was despatched by Joan rather quickly and abruptly. Our unplanned, final session came in late January, when the crocuses were starting to peep through, the daylight hours were stretching out longer in the afternoon and the garden was beginning to fill with birdsong. Joan had chosen her new, adapted car and, with her compromised hand now raised proudly above shoulder level, she told me she was feeling so much brighter and able to cope. This felt like an authentic and, more importantly, empowered decision.

Together we reviewed what we had explored in our sessions and what Joan had learnt about herself. We focused in on the strategies and experiences that she would carry within her as her own internal counsellor when life brought its difficulties in the future. As we ended, Joan showed me a postcard that had come that day with a picture of a lady with white hair and a cheeky grin pulling an airport trolley piled impossibly high with luggage. She then produced her cruise brochures and announced that, with her car coming, it was time for a new adventure.

In working with the ageing, elderly and profoundly old, the challenge is to look beyond the perceived limitations – beyond the greying hair, lack of independence, restricted mobility, loss of bodily strength, reliance on others, cognitive impairment, poor eyesight or hearing – and see and nurture the unique human being in the room. The challenge is not to regard these limitations as weaknesses or barriers to a lively, healing encounter. I was profoundly impacted by sociologist Laura Carstensen, whose TED talk titled 'Older People Are Happier' (2011) changed how I viewed the paradigm of the ageing society. She argues, based on sound research, that as we age, we can become increasingly influential and achieve more than in our youth because we can handle conflict better and have more patience, more life experience and are generally happier (Carstensen, 2009). She finished the talk with a quote from her 92-year-old father: 'Let's stop talking only about how to save the old folks and start talking about how to get them to save us all.' If anyone can take the lead on this, my money is on Joan.

References

Birren JE, Lubben JE, Rowe JC, Deutchman DE (1991). *The Concept and Measurement of Quality of Life in the Frail Elderly.* San Diego, CA: Academic Press.

Bott D, Howard P (2012). *The Therapeutic Encounter: a cross-modality approach*. London: Sage Publications.

Bowlby E (1969/1997). *Attachment and Loss. Vol 1: Attachment*. London: Pimlico.

Bronfenbrenner U (1993). Ecological models of human development. In: Gauvain M, Cole M (eds). *Readings on the Development of Children* (2nd ed). New York, NY: Freeman (pp37–43).

Campbell D (2017). Loneliness as bad for health as long-term illness, says GPs' chief. [Online.] *Guardian*; 27 November.

Carstensen L (2011). *Older People are Happier*. TEDx Women 2011; December. www.ted.com/talks/laura_carstensen_older_people_are_happier (accessed 18 December 2018).

Carstensen L (2009). *A Long Bright Future*. New York, NY: Broadway Books.

Clarkson, P (1989). *Gestalt Counselling in Action*. London: Sage.

Erikson JM, Erikson EH (1997). *The Life Cycle Completed: a review*. New York, NY: WW Norton & Company.

Grieder A (2002). Solitude: a phenomenological approach. In: du Plock S (ed). *Further Existential Challenges to the Psychotherapeutic Theory and Practice: papers from Existential Analysis*. London: Society for Existential Practice (pp226–237).

Mearns D, Cooper M (2005). *Working at Relational Depth in Counselling and Psychotherapy*. London: Sage Publications.

Rapp H (2000). Working with difference. In: Lawton B, Feltham C (eds). *Taking Supervision Forward: enquiries and trends in counselling and psychotherapy*. London: Sage Publications (pp93–112).

Rogers CR (1951/2003). *Client-Centred Therapy*. London: Constable.

Scrutton S (1999). *Counselling Older People* (2nd ed). London: Arnold.

Stern D (1985). *The Interpersonal World of the Infant*. New York, NY: Basic Books.

Stern DN (1998). The process of therapeutic change involving implicit knowledge: some implications of developmental observations for adult psychotherapy. *Infant Mental Health Journal 19*(3): 300–308.

Spinelli E (2007). *Practising Existential Therapy: the relational world*. London: Sage Publications.

Tolkein JRR (2002). *The Lord of the Rings*. London: HarperCollins.

Tornstam L (1997). Gerotranscendence: the contemplative dimension of aging. *Journal of Aging Studies 11*(2): 143–154.

Van Deurzen-Smith E (2012). *Existential Counselling and Psychotherapy in Practice* (3rd ed). London: Sage Publications.

Her indoors
Kate

'I don't want to know what other people have told you about
yourself, I want to know about you.'
Eleanor Longden, *The Voices in My Head*

'Would you like a foxglove for your garden?'

Here it is, the moment when a counsellor feels their internal
supervisor sitting up and paying attention. What would it mean for
the client if I accepted – or didn't accept? How would it be for me
to have a little bit of my client's world growing in my own garden?
Should we explore this together before I decide?

In fact, the remarkable part of this moment was none of these
things; it was the fact that this home-bound, agoraphobic and severely
anxious lady was able to tolerate our being outside at all and had, to
an extent, begun to come alive in her drafty, cluttered greenhouse in a
way I hadn't seen before. The possibility of something new happening
was both actual and metaphorical. We were sowing seeds and taking
off-shoots, and she had taken a tiny step out into the world that
terrified her. 'Yes please!' I answered impulsively, 'I love foxgloves.
Thank you.'

And I do, as did my grandma. They remind me of her and of
her garden and her love of gardening. This is where the similarities
stop but it is worth noting. I often wonder how my own experiences
of my grandparents influences my work with my elderly clients. I

find, even as I write this, that my immediate reaction is a concern that, by even thinking this, I am somehow lumping all elderly people together as a 'type'. However, if our early experiences of our main, parental caregivers are so influential on how we interact with others, it is surely inevitable that our early experiences of our grandparents imprint an experience or response to older people when we are adults. Certainly, our experiences of older people who were important in our lives must impact on our sense of self and identity when we become elderly ourselves. I think this is worth reflecting on if we choose to work with older adults. In fact, in his own extensive research on octogenarians, Erikson noted this as one element he earlier omitted from his life cycle theory (Erikson, Erikson & Kivnick, 1989).

Both my maternal and paternal grandmothers lived well into their 90s and were sociable, independent, confident ladies, having survived their husbands by many years. I learnt as a child and into my early adulthood, by simply being around them, that ladies over the age of 80 can carve out their own identity beyond widowhood, continue to contribute to their community and make independent choices about what is right for them. My existential orientation as a counsellor means I believe choices are always available to us, no matter how stuck or confined we feel. With clients of any age, I consider it part of our work together to notice what aspects of their life are not serving them and look for the possibility of something different.

On a long train journey, while I was writing this book, I found myself sitting opposite two women in their late 70s and early 80s respectively who, it turned out, both volunteered as counsellors. The perfect symmetry of this chance encounter was not lost on me. During our conversation, one of the ladies remarked that her mantra was, 'I am retired from work, but not from life.'

'So many people seem to think that retirement is wholesale. I don't accept that,' she told me. They both went on to say that their recommendation to people approaching old age was to actively take risks. I raised my eyebrows, questioningly. 'Well, it's the opposite of what is expected but it keeps you feeling young and keeps you growing,' she said. These two wonderful ladies, whose station arrived far too early for me, epitomised what I had learned from my own grandmothers about living out the later stages of life.

Returning to Kate in her greenhouse – she was small, almost bird-like, with piercing eyes, and had been widowed 18 months before we met. She lived alone in the four-bedroomed house where she had spent 44 years of married life with her husband, George. On a table beside her chair, she kept her diary, in which she had written down her plans for each day, right down to the individual household chores. Alongside her diary was a clutch of paperwork, newspaper cuttings, leaflets she had been given and important letters. She had everything to hand.

Kate was 80 years old and had two adult children, each with families of their own, who lived close by. She had suffered with periods of agoraphobia and wasn't involved in any friendship or social groups. This much I knew from the referral. She told me when we met that all her friends but one were dead and she had no immediate surviving relatives other than her son and daughter and their families.

Since Kate didn't drive, our sessions took place in her home, as with other clients. In our early sessions I had to consider whether my visiting her perpetuated her habit of staying in the safety of her home and if it might mean we missed an opportunity for her to venture safely into new environments. This is very hard to gauge at a first conversation or meeting; my preference is to note my own process and what might be the process of the client in agreeing where we meet, and to negotiate and explore these as we progress through our work together.

As our sessions progressed and more of Kate's life experiences and narrative emerged, I noticed that she had spent her entire life within what appeared to be a radius of between five and 10 miles around where she lived. My private counselling room was 18 miles from her house and, for her, it might as well have been on the moon. Kate grew up with five siblings in a house just a few streets away from where she now lived. Her father was in a clerical job and her mother looked after the children and the house. Kate attended a secondary school that was a short walk from her home and her children attended a neighbouring secondary school many years later. She lived at home after leaving school, attended secretarial college and got her first job in the town. She moved out of her parents' home when she married George, whom she met at a dance and fell in love with the same night. They bought their first family home not far from that of her parents and their two children were born over the next five years. They then moved to a new, bigger, detached house just streets away from their first, and there they stayed for the next 44 years. Kate never learnt to drive ('Well, you didn't then'). Her life was caring for her children and George and keeping the house. Holidays were taken in their touring caravan in local campsites. For the last few years of George's life, Kate cared for him at home until, in 2016, he died suddenly, in his sleep, next to her in bed. Kate's initial presenting issue was persistent low mood and a feeling of being stuck in her grief. Her goal in seeking counselling, which her children had suggested, was to be able to go about her old routine again and to find enjoyment in it.

Usually, it takes a few sessions for me to start to build a picture of what might be happening between me and the client in the room and how this might be shaped by the life experiences that they bring forward in our sessions. Exploring that allows me to start to feel into what might be holding us back and how we can begin to open the possibility of something different. Very early on in my sessions with Kate, a word that emerged in my head was 'enmeshment'. Initially I noticed the closeness (physical and emotional) of her children, whose views and activities she frequently mentioned, and her routine, maintained religiously, of visiting each of them once a week, every week. Kate told me of two breakdowns that she had experienced in her life: one following the birth of her second child and the other after the breakdown of her daughter's marriage. When she described her own childhood, she talked of her close bonds with her siblings and her mother, of staying at home until her marriage, and of caring for her mother, who lived in a care home nearby until her death.

However, I am always mindful of the cultural and temporal differences between the here-and-now of the 2010s and the there-and-then of the 1920s and 1930s. Karpen (Wyatt-Brown, Karpen & Kivnick, 2016) states that we close the gap between observer and observed by staying phenomenological. Laing, in spite of his energetic attempt to stay close to an understanding of client experience, conceded that a 'kernel' of the client's experience always remains incomprehensible to the clinician (Laing, 1960). As with any client, I find the best way to stay close to clients' lived experiences is to ask them to tell me about the personal, particular details of their lives. In this way I avoid imprinting my own cultural paradigm on them by constructing their past through a sepia-tinted lens, like some movie conjured from the conceit of my relative youth.

Therefore, while on the surface I sensed an intergenerational family environment of being close and having shared life experiences, what I was missing was an appreciation of the cultural normality of living one's entire life within a small family unit within a small market town. My life had taken a different path. It is highly probable that a female born in the 1970s and educated through the 1980s and 1990s will have left home at 18, sought further education in a place much further away, and then pursued a career yet somewhere else, never returning to the family home town. The freedom and funds to travel widely and have new experiences outside the familiar was, for most, beyond the grasp of our parents and grandparents. Taking the Bronfenbrenner model of human development (1993), this is how the chronosystem of time and place can shape a person. My reflections on Kate's early familial situation were informed by the time and place I was born into. As we talked in more detail, it became apparent, conversely, that Kate prized the closeness of her family, but also saw it as unremarkable, normal.

In supervision, I was able to play this out a little and was encouraged instead to look for stories that were not yet ready to be articulated. In his work, Spinelli (2007) challenges us never to pre-judge who is right or wrong. What made it so hard for Kate to consider leaving the house or breaking her routine? What made it hard for her to do things without her family, of which there now survived so few? It seemed so challenging for her to think of a single thing she could do that was new and different, even when we explored this gently as part of our work. I had a strong feeling that her identity was so caught up in being with or caring for others in her family that, left alone as she was now, without many dependents, she found the idea of having her own identity dizzyingly disorientating. I, conversely, found myself feeling excited about the possibility of us exploring it together.

Writing about self-actualisation, Abraham Maslow suggested our true, inner self will always be heard, even if it speaks in the softest voice, and this 'essential core' (1968) needs to be recognised by others for it to come forward. He suggests that what causes neurosis is evading or obscuring our core self. It was by accident one day that we saw a closer glimpse of Kate's true, individual self, not the one that was tethered to or obscured by others.

Kate was showing me a black-and-white photo of George and telling me about when they met.

'My brother was going to a dance. I loved dancing and was really quite good at it and he asked me to go with him. It worked well as it meant he could walk me home. I loved dances, but I hated the way you had to choose someone to dance with. I just loved dancing! And I wasn't the type to get swept off my feet.'

'No?'

'No, well, it's embarrassing really, but I was the one who acted more like the boys did. If I saw one I liked, we might dance together and they might walk me home, but it was me who decided if we would see each other again. I was a bit of a devil like that.'

Kate's face had changed in this moment. Her eyes, usually suspicious and squinting a little, sparkled and widened. She smiled openly and leaned in towards me as she spoke, in a conspiratorial way. We laughed together as she described these times and I told her how different she seemed to be in that moment. I wondered out loud to her, where was this this confident girl now who, at a time when other girls were ready to be swept off their feet, danced with whom she liked and when she liked?

The answer to this question, as it eventually emerged, was complex and layered with personal, medical and cultural factors. I found myself wondering what might not have emerged yet, what story wasn't yet being told, and how to get towards a more realistic narrative so that Kate had a chance to nurture an individual identity back to life after so many years as wife, mother and carer.

With Kate, the opportunity to do this presented itself, as it often does, through a tiny crack in her narrative. She had noticed an advert in the paper for a new retirement community and we'd been talking about it in our sessions. We got on to talking about the family home where she still lived, where our sessions were taking place.

Kate sighed: 'Moving here was a big enough move, George was so nervous about it, but his friends were saying we had all this money now from his business, so we should treat ourselves to something bigger.'

I registered, silently for now, the first mention of George's anxiety. Up until now, Kate was the one in the relationship who had been portrayed as fearful and anxious. 'You wanted to move here?' I asked.

'Oh yes, and the girls were so happy to have the big garden and a bedroom each. It made sense.'

'But George wasn't sure…'

A pause. I waited.

'No, and he was depressed for a while when we first moved here. He didn't like change. He liked his routine. He would never think about moving to a place like this one in the paper.'

Kate was still holding the newspaper cutting in her hand, with its pictures of bright, well-appointed apartments and a smart, subsidised restaurant. I wondered how George might have approached the idea of moving again, were he here, and, more importantly, how differently Kate might be feeling about it now that it was her choice.

This would be difficult to navigate. Cooper says that when we come up against deeply sedimented beliefs they will feel almost primal and very difficult to challenge (2003). He encourages us to notice them but to go carefully with challenging them, as they are there for a reason. The reality of working with elderly clients who seek counselling is that the loss of a partner is often uppermost in what is being felt or talked about. If we go back to the cultural nuances of a generation that married early and, in many cases, for life, then the deceased partner is often given much of the focus in counselling sessions. Whether it was a happy marriage or not, it is often very hard to explore with the client a more realistic view of the partner who has died. Dying often reifies the deceased. Long-held narratives of a happy, perfect life together are precious and, in my experience of them in the counselling room, difficult to challenge.

Added to this, many of this generation married when they were quite young, so much of their growing up took place within the relationship. Up until 1970, the average age of marriage was 24 for women and 27 for men (Office for National Statistics, 2016). For those marrying in 1960, the divorce rate is less than 30%, compared with 45% for those who married between 1990 and 1995 (Marriage Foundation, 2016). Moreover, longer marriages are linked with longer life: research finds that couples who have been married for 50 years are more than 200 times more likely to live to 100 than those who get divorced. Finding an identity that stands alone from a life partner can feel like a betrayal and can be frightening and difficult to achieve.

At this point I am going to take a step back and talk about how I experienced Kate's engagement with me. One of the things I had noticed early on was that routine and expectations were very important to her. One week, I asked if we might meet slightly later in the day. Kate seemed to find this change difficult; she 'knew where she was' with our 9.30am meeting. When we originally arranged our regular sessions, our negotiations centred around avoiding disruption to mealtimes (breakfast regularly at 8am, lunch at 11.30am and dinner at 4.30pm) and the daily chores she set herself, all documented in her diary. It transpired that the mealtimes had been that way for years, as they fitted into George's work schedule. Kate had continued this routine in the 18 months since his death, without question, but it had not felt at all comforting or enjoyable without him. Yet, deviating from this routine, when we explored it, felt very difficult for her to do.

Kate's goal for counselling was to 'get back to her old routine and to enjoy it', remember; it was not to reintegrate with life after her husband's death or to try something new. Indeed, it was very far from that: understandably, her goal was to keep George close and present by continuing to live out their routine together, regardless of whether it still served her now. As I thought back to the late teenager that Kate had described and whom I had seen momentarily in her eyes, I felt something different might be possible for her. I began to wonder if anxiety, routine and fear of the new had been, to a certain extent, experiences that had evolved with George, during their 44 years together. What, I wondered, might it be like for Kate to find a little bit of autonomy and freedom from that?

What I hadn't considered or encountered yet were all the elements that held her back. George was only one of them. Counsellors are in the privileged position of being invited into the private, intimate world of our clients and to walk with them within it. However, we enter into these worlds as human beings, with our own set of experiences. This often means that, while we are fellow travellers across our clients' inner landscapes, we have considerable blind spots. These can be created by our own experiences, by a client's defence mechanisms, by environmental factors or socio-political influences.

Hence, I feel that it is important to consider, when working with older adults, that meaning-making can have its roots in time and within a socio-cultural context that is very different to our own. It is our responsibility to try to bridge the gap. A client's relationship with their distress or a specific diagnosis they have received must always be explored carefully, in my experience, paying close attention to meaning and context, otherwise we risk making assumptions, consciously or otherwise.

I was getting a sense of how Kate's life might be different, but we had not yet explored what, specifically, was causing life to be so intolerable to her. We got to it, eventually, more due to my frustration than anything else.

'I am wondering what it is about going about your old routine that leaves you feeling so unhappy.'

'It's just not the same…'

'No.'

'… because, obviously, I'm depressed.'

'You feel depressed.'

'Well, I've been told I've got depression.'

This was said through tight lips and she looked down and smoothed out the creases on her skirt.

'Who tells you this, Kate?' I lowered my head to try and meet her gaze.

'The doctor told me when she gave me the medication and the girls tell me I'm depressed too, so I must be, mustn't I?'

Pause.

'… and, I mean, depression runs right through my family. All of my siblings struggled, three of them were on medication at some point, and both my girls suffer with depression too from time to time.'

Another pause.

'Kate, I can hear a lot about everyone else, but I am struggling to hear what your experience of all of this is.'

She looked at me blankly.

Mental ill health and emotional distress were taboo subjects in the 1960s when Kate's generation was coming into adulthood. In 1961, the then Minister of Health, Enoch Powell, announced at the AGM of the National Association for Mental Health that the government planned to close the majority of mental health institutions, most originating from the 1880s, that were designed both to give asylum to those in mental distress and to separate them from society. However, it took another 25 years for these closures and attempts to reintegrate their inmates into the community to begin. Community care and talking therapy with the range and access that we have today were non-existent. For the over-75-year-old generation, manifestations of mental distress still carry a stigma of exclusion and 'otherness'. Responses to mental health diagnoses and to talking therapy can also be coloured by these attitudes. I almost missed these cultural markers when I was working with Kate; this was my blind spot, as it were.

I felt like I was pushing against a tide of opinion and I wanted to try and navigate us to her experience, not the experiences of others.

'What is it like for you?'

'Well, I was all right for 11 months after George died, you know. I was coping and getting on with everything every day and then it just hit me one day. The shock wore off and I had palpitations and I was crying.'

'You were in shock and doing OK and then it wore off and you felt very sad.' I felt I wanted to reflect back her experiences as she had described them, to keep close to her experiences, not what others had told her.

'Yes, and I suddenly felt like I couldn't cope. I read about the grief process and it says that doesn't it? That you cope for a while and then everything comes crashing down later when the shock wears off. Well, then the girls told me they didn't like seeing me so upset and took me to the doctor, who said I was depressed and gave me the tablets. She said they would help me out a bit.'

The tablets were amitriptyline, one of a class of medications called tricyclic antidepressants that are used to improve mood and feelings of wellbeing and relieve anxiety and tension. Kate described how she had taken them for a bit but had to come off them as she had so many side effects that they had become counterproductive. I must confess that I felt a familiar flash of irritation that Kate had gone to the doctors with symptoms of grief and was sent away with medication. But what interested me more was that she felt so comfortable in acquiescing with what other people thought and said, as though she had no autonomy to challenge it. Indeed, her involuntary response to any statements I made was always: 'Do you think so?'

I am inspired by the stance of existential therapy on deconstructing assumptions (van Deurzen, 2012) and believe this can happen through close, moment-to-moment attention within the therapeutic relationship. In her work on life passages, Sheehy (1995) encourages us to try to grow with every transition we go through in life. She makes the point that people who flourish are those who toss out the old expectations of ageing. 'With each passage of human growth, we must shed a protective structure. We are left exposed and vulnerable – but also yeasty and embryonic again, capable of stretching in ways we hadn't known before.' This was a significant period of transition for Kate: from wife to widowhood, from her eighth to her ninth decade of life. In fact, grief itself is a very significant transition, one that demands that those left behind reframe their way of being in the world without the person who has died (Murray-Parkes, 2008). How could Kate and I break out of acquiescence and into an authentic strategy for her to live with her grief and enjoy her life?

I wondered too how I might liberate Kate from the story of herself that she so frequently heard from others. It could be said that those who consider themselves to be elderly live out their own lives according to others' stories about the elderly. In her book on personal construct therapy with the elderly, Linda Viney (1993) advocates allowing people to tell and retell their story until they find the one that is right for them. In this way, they can, perhaps, liberate their story from those of others.

'... Kate, do you think you are depressed?'

'Well, I know *you* don't think I am because you said you wouldn't tell me that.'

'I want us to try and stay with how you feel, if we can, rather than what I or anyone else think... What does it feel like for you?'

'I want George back! I don't want to live the next however many years without him. Every minute of every day I think about him and wish he was here. I can't cope!'

Here, her voice broke and she cried a little.

'Life is very hard without George.'

'Yes,' emphatically, 'and I can't cope.'

'... and you don't feel you can cope.'

'Well, whenever I feel sad and cry or have my heart palpitations, the girls get upset and say they don't like to see me like that, you know, and they tell me we should see the doctor.'

'We,' I emphasised.

'Well, the girls have to take me as I don't drive, that is what I mean.'

Kate paused and thought. 'And when I see the doctor, they try to give me new tablets or send me for tests on my heart. Well, I know there's nothing wrong with my heart as I've been tested!'

'Yes.' I took a breath. 'Kate, I'm afraid I don't buy it. I think it is maybe others who think you can't cope.'

I leaned forward for emphasis and locked eyes with her deliberately.

Kate blinked at me: 'Do you really think so?'

'I hear you are grieving, I hear life is hard, but I also see that you are functioning and living your life as best you can.'

'Oh.'

Needless to say, I took this moment to supervision. I am still not sure what prompted me to be so direct; as soon as the words left my mouth and she made her small 'Oh' in response, I experienced a post-climactic rush of doubt. Was this too much? But I know that, in that exact moment, I was passionately committed to Kate and to creating something new for her.

Kate's response took me by surprise. There was a small pause and she shifted position slightly and held my gaze: 'I do wish you were my friend.'

It felt on the surface to be utterly incongruous with what had preceded it; we could have a field day theoretically exploring the transference or the projections within it. However, it was expressed factually, not wistfully or in a manipulative way. Revisiting the theory of relational depth, Mearns (Mearns & Cooper, 2005) proposed that, in such moments the client and therapist cannot lie; there is no transference or countertransference. Indeed, I felt no pull of pre-guilt about our inevitable ending and no desire to kindly reiterate the message about boundaries. I simply let the words sit between us and nodded.

Before I pat myself on the back, metaphorically, I was also in some way telling Kate what to believe. However, we had at least moved past the 'can't cope' narrative into something different. The impassioned therapist in me was cantering ahead, wondering what it would be like if Kate believed she could cope. What could it be like for her to own her experience and trust how she felt? Even my supervisor had been seduced by this, and we had explored the strength of the pull to nurture this part of her. However, brilliantly and rightly, Kate navigated towards her own meaning and therapeutic outcome from this encounter, leaving mine in its wake.

It wasn't until our next session that the ripples of this tiny therapeutic moment began to gain momentum and, as I said, not in the way that you or I might expect. It is worth at this point reiterating some details of Kate's life that she had shared in our sessions. At the age of 12, Kate had been told by a school nurse that she had a lung condition, because she sometimes became out of breath in PE. She was subsequently treated differently to her peers: she didn't have to take part in physical education and she didn't go on school trips and other such activities. By age 16, Kate was experiencing what she now knew to be agoraphobia attacks. She continued to cycle to and from school but acutely remembered moments of crippling fear when she was out in open spaces. At the age of 40, in 1978, Kate suffered what she called a nervous breakdown. She told me that, following a walk in the woods with her children at the end of the school term, she returned to find her husband packing to take them camping for the weekend as a surprise. She took to the sofa, paralysed by fear, and ended up in hospital for four weeks. She had not experienced any further significant episodes until the death of her beloved husband 18 months ago.

In our next session, during a moment of quiet, Kate suddenly offered: 'I was thinking what you said about me coping and I suppose I coped alone with my agoraphobia for most of my life. I had no choice.'

'Yes. Can you tell me more about that?' I said.

'Well, when I went to the doctor with it back then, he told me he was pretty sure I had agoraphobia and that there was nothing that could be done about it, I just had to live with it. I just had no choice. It was awful but there you are, there was nothing to be done.'

'And you said you coped,' I encouraged.

'Well, I worked out ways, you know, to make it as bearable as I could. I had to cycle to school and back twice a day in those days and then I did the same when I got my job in the bank. I didn't have a choice, you see? So, I would choose a route that meant I could be under trees or in more enclosed spaces. If I got an attack, I would stop and start breathing deeply until it went.'

'It sounds like you were able to find your own strategies, Kate.'

'Yes, well, I did. And then once I got married and didn't have to work anymore – we had to resign from our jobs in those days when we got married, you see – I could be at home and it was easier. But I still went out and it was OK as long as I was under trees, so we used to walk in the woods over there, you know.'

'So, you coped with your phobia without much support.'

'Yes, well, until I was in hospital after my breakdown. Then I was on the medication, you know.'

No, I didn't know, but the clues had been there, and I had been somewhat blind to them. Kate kept a bag by her at all times, and often brought out her tablets and their boxes and leaflets when she talked about her visits to the doctor. She'd previously told me that she'd been prescribed the benzodiazepine Lorazepam, a sedative used to treat fast-onset panic anxiety, along with a number of other problems such as seizures and insomnia. I had wrongly assumed this was for the palpitations she had experienced since her husband's death.

I kept still and silent to allow her space.

'When I left hospital, I was given Lorazepam, so I could cope with being at home. They have helped with the agoraphobia.'

'You are taking Lorazepam at the moment?'

'Yes, I've taken them for 40 years.'

'Since you left hospital back then.' My surprise was evident in my voice and expression.

'Yes.'

The early 1960s saw the advent of the medicalisation of emotional and psychological distress. One piece of recent research, based on extensive records of a mental health institute in Brussels, found that, in 1969, 86% of patients were receiving medication, compared with 24% in 1950 (Majerus, 2016). The same study also showed, from first-hand patient and nurse accounts, the increasing acceptance and awareness of patients that these drugs were part of their healing process. Over subsequent decades, their use and visibility extended far beyond the reach of the institution and into society (Majerus, 2016). The modern pharmaceutical industry was being born. By the time Kate was hospitalised in the late 1970s, treatment with medication for anxiety and panic attacks would be normal. From Kate's account, it appears that her phobia and resulting anxiety was managed largely by medication in the latter half of her life. It is hardly surprising that, when grief broke through the barrier of the tranquilisers, neither she, nor those around her, knew how to react.

As a humanistic, existential counsellor, one doesn't make an analysis. You may wonder and explore possibilities, but you don't infer and impose meaning on a client. However, at this point, every part of me put two and two together and found four, fuelled I suspect by my own views on the medicalisation of distress. Kate had developed effective coping strategies in her early life, and then, later in life, when her fear threatened to engulf her, she was offered medication. And perhaps medication had kept her fear and strong emotions at bay for 40 years. I was angry, but was this *my* anger?

'Kate, do you know, I notice that I am feeling angry that you have taken this medication for so long when you had some coping strategies you were already using.'

'Yes, well, I'm not angry, it kind of makes sense. But I wish I didn't have to take them, I suppose. I tried to come off them last year, but it was a disaster, I felt awful.'

In some ways the anger I felt was mine and it was political. As a counsellor, I sometimes feel like a tiny insurgent in a world hell-bent on medicalising every human condition that departs from the smooth-running, acceptable norm. As the medical model of mental illness continues its imperialist march across the globe (Doward, 2016; James & Douglas, 2013), I regard counselling as occupying a tiny microcosm at odds with the macrocosm of this world (Bronfenbrenner, 1993). People break down for complex, unique, psychosocial reasons, and so we can explore and heal these breakdowns by exploring those same reasons, not simply with standardised or medicine-dominated approaches (Laing, 1960).

Foucault wrote, in *The Birth of the Clinic* (1973), that patients and their illnesses only exist through a 'medical gaze' and in this way we obscure the complex, individualised meanings of their condition. Such a way of viewing distress 'was not the perception of the patient in his singularity, but a collective consciousness, with all the information that intersects in it, growing in a complex, ever-proliferating way until it finally achieves the dimensions of a history, a geography, a state' (p29). In considering Kate in supervision, I became aware that illness and distress formed the frame through which she was seen by her family and doctor and that she had been seen that way for most of her life. I considered the way she kept her bag of tablets and leaflets close by her; I considered the connection between her misdiagnosed lung condition and her subsequent phobia, and I considered that she had been given the labels for her experiences: depression, agoraphobia. And, in writing this, I notice that this account differs from the other chapters: is there less Kate and more narrative, theory and research? Is she getting lost again? My anger at her medicalisation was of little use to our relationship or to her. I was just another person telling her story; how could I get her to craft her own?

As I write this account, I notice the number of times I have made value or truth statements about Kate and her life. I notice that I am keen to hold onto some certainties; I quote statistics and provide medical information. In short, I move from reflecting on the feeling and experiencing within our encounter towards certainty and facts, and my sense is that this was within the transferential invitation from

Kate: she was calling on me to be a certain way with her, but she wasn't doing this consciously or deliberately; it was habitual and outside her awareness. Kate was showing me how it was to be living her life: a life where others' opinions, medication and routine formed the structure of her experience. How interesting that the ripple effect of what is co-created between client and therapist, which is often replicated and explored within supervision, can also ripple outward into the process of writing about clients, as I feel it has here.

There is no happy-ever-after denouement to this account of my work with Kate. It was supposed to end after the six sessions permitted by the organisation for which I worked, and time was already feeling woefully short. I had negotiated two further sessions and, in the three sessions we had left, we planned together to move towards reflecting on the coping mechanisms that she had used many years before and that had worked for her, to try and find some confidence in her own abilities. Spring was finally starting to make an appearance and we had made plans for more planting in the garden. My hope was that we had challenged together her construct that she 'couldn't cope' and re-imagined it as 'I can find my own ways of coping'.

The day before our sixth session, I received a voice message from Kate's daughter, letting me know that Kate was feeling unwell and wouldn't be up to our session. The following week, two days before our regular session, her daughter called again and left a message: 'Mum is not feeling so well at the moment. We have been to the doctor and the doctor feels the counselling isn't a good idea for her as it is bringing up things that are difficult. Thank you, but she doesn't want to have any more sessions.'

My immediate response was shock and tears. I felt reprimanded; I felt that I had been told to be quiet. My next concern was a professional one: the BACP ethical framework asks us to act with beneficence, to do no harm to our clients (2018). The phone message had left me feeling that our work had made things worse for Kate. I felt profound sadness. To ensure that the ending was clear and boundaried, I called her number back. Kate answered the phone. I could hear someone else talking in the background.

'Kate, hello, it's Helen.'

'Oh hello.' ('It's Helen,' she explained to the other person.)

'Kate, I just got a message from your daughter that you'd like to finish our sessions. Is that right?'

'Yes, well, it seems to be the right thing. They were very early in the day anyway and I couldn't get on with that and it's Easter coming up and you will be busy and I want to get myself better.'

None of this sounded to me terribly rational or like the real reason, but I needed to respect Kate's autonomy and choice. So I checked in once more.

'OK, so I hear the sessions are difficult for you for lots of reasons. Would you like to continue once Easter is over or leave it completely?'

'I think it's best to leave it, thank you. You've been very helpful, but I think it's time to stop.'

Endings create such powerful emotions; sometimes it is relief, sometimes it is frustration, but this time I felt profoundly sad. I can account for that in two ways: first, because, despite talking to her and hearing her own words rather than those of her daughter, part of me felt she was acquiescing out of duty to others; second, because I valued our time together and felt that we had both been silenced. Truly, there was something a little sinister about the presence of her daughter during our call. It was hard to have the ending we might have had were we in the room together within a therapeutic space. In my fantasy, she was watching what she said, and I was definitely filtering what I said.

So, I simply told the truth: 'I will miss our sessions,' I told her.

'Oh.'

'Please know that you can come back to me at any time if anything changes.'

'OK, thank you.'

'Goodbye, Kate.'

'Bye-bye, then.'

And that was that. I like to think that, if nothing else, our sessions reintroduced Kate to her teenage and younger self and to the notion that she could find her own ways of coping with what was happening for her. My hope is that these tiny seeds, given some water and light, continued to grow, like the foxglove in my garden.

References

BACP (2018). *Ethical Framework for the Counselling Professions.* Lutterworth: BACP. www.bacp.co.uk/events-and-resources/ethics-and-standards/ethical-framework-for-the-counselling-professions (accessed 1 December 2018).

Bronfenbrenner U (1993). Ecological models of human development. In: Gauvain M, Cole M (eds). *Readings on the Development of Children* (2nd ed). New York, NY: Freeman (pp37–43).

Cooper M (2003). *Existential Therapies.* London: Sage Publications.

Doward J (2013). Medicine's big new battleground: does mental illness really exist? [Online.] *The Observer*; 12 May. www.theguardian.com/society/2013/may/12/medicine-dsm5-row-does-mental-illness-exist (accessed 21 March 2018).

Erikson EH, Erikson JM, Kivnick HQ (1989). *Vital Involvement in Old Age.* New York, NY: WW Norton& Co.

Foucault M (1973). *The Birth of the Clinic: an archaeology of medical perception.* London: Tavistock Publications.

James P, Douglas B (2013). *Common Presenting Issues in Psychotherapeutic Practice.* London: Sage Publications.

Karpen RR (2016). Coming to care. In: Wyatt-Brown AM, Karpen RR, Kivnick HQ. *The Big Move: life between turning points.* Bloomington, IN: Indiana University Press (pp29–39).

Laing RD (1960). *The Divided Self: an existential study in sanity and madness.* London: Tavistock Publications.

Longden E (2013). *Learning from the Voices in My Head.* TED Books Book 9. [Kindle edition.] TED Conferences.

Majerus B (2016). Making sense of the 'chemical revolution': patients' voices on the introduction of neuroleptics in the 1950s. *Medical History 60*(1): 54–56.

Marriage Foundation (2016). *Establishing the facts about family breakdown and transforming the debate about marriage.* Briefing note. [Online.] Marriage Foundation. http://marriagefoundation.org.uk/research (accessed 1 December 2018).

Maslow AH (1968). *Toward a Psychology of Being* (2nd ed). New York, NY: Van Nostrand Reinhold.

Mearns D, Cooper M (2005). *Working at Relational Depth in Counselling and Psychotherapy.* London: Sage Publications.

Murray-Parkes C (2008). *Love and Loss: the roots of grief and its complications.* London: Routledge.

Office for National Statistics (2016). *Marriages in England and Wales: 2013. Statistical bulletin.* [Online.] ONS. www.ons.gov.uk/peoplepopulationandcommunity/birthsdeathsandmarriages/marriagecohabitationandcivilpartnerships/bulletins/marriagesinenglandandwalesprovisional/2013 (accessed 21 March 2018).

Sheehy G (1995). *New Passages: mapping your life across time*. New York, NY: Random House.

Spinelli E (2007). *Practising Existential Therapy: the relational world*. London: Sage Publications.

Van Deurzen E (2012). *Existential Counselling and Psychotherapy in Practice* (3rd ed). London: Sage Publications.

Viney L (1993). *Life Stories*. Chichester: Wiley.

The dolls' house
Alice

'Memories warm you up from the inside. But they also tear you apart.'
Haruki Murakami, *Kafka on the Shore*

One Sunday, watching a game of rugby, wrapped up against the inclement elements, I happened to check my emails on my phone. Among the spam and notifications, I noticed an email from a client. I skimmed its contents, reminding myself to read it again properly next day when back at work, then felt myself physically flinch against a familiar contraction of anger in my abdomen, which slowly faded to shame and then sadness. A profoundly old client, whom I had met for the first time a few days ago, had decided not to progress with counselling.

'I feel that going back and talking in depth would not be in my interest,' he'd written. 'I am sure there are often instances of unanswered questions when people die and sometimes they are best left to rest.' The visceral reaction I'd had to this email was out of proportion to its contents and to the depth of our therapeutic relationship. I registered at the time that it was something I would need to process, but the sadness stayed with me all day, clouding my experiences and conversations. I felt confused and I noticed myself questioning how I practise. It wasn't the first time this happened; it wouldn't be the last, but it was significant.

Practising as a therapist is a complex journey of discovery, development, reflection, self-awareness, crippling disappointment and fist-pumping moments of euphoria. Each encounter with a client asks us to commit all of ourselves, plunging us into a tumult of emotions and experiences that change us. In the reflective and heuristic writing of this book, I have noticed that the parallel processes of clinical practice and writing become intimately entangled, with similar complications. As counsellors make themselves open to the unpredictability of being transformed by others (Cooper, 2003), so, I have come to believe, those who write can expect the writing process itself will change them.

The BACP ethical framework (2018) asks therapists to make clients our primary concern while we are working with them and to practise self-care. To do this, we undertake supervision and personal therapy and use reflective techniques to constantly account for our prejudices and any personal experiences that might impact our ability to be in the service of our clients. To a certain extent, the writing of this book is one long reflective process. However, writing about therapy can also have the reverse effect. I see this as an ever-decreasing circle of feedback: I engage in some work that I reflect upon and write about; I read more to inform, challenge and reinforce my practice; I feel I 'know' more and become impassioned and inspired; I engage in some more work with what I feel is a new sense of understanding of what might facilitate growth. This can expand my experience but, it seems, conversely also reduce it, by moving it out of an immediate, felt sense and into a cognitive one. The process of putting an experience into print somehow provides the illusion of certainty and makes it harder to hold onto a position of ignorant wonder at what is unfolding.

Many of these chapters describe moments of awareness that hold the potential for change. In Chapter 2, we met Bobby, whose release from his guilt about his childhood abuse, 75 years after the event, allowed him to reimagine his life narrative. In Chapter 3, Joan and I eventually found a way to welcome her emotions into our sessions, after her lifelong obeisance to the law of the stiff upper lip. Of course, as a counsellor, I am only invited into someone's world for a short time, usually one hour a week for several weeks, or perhaps months. What happens after our work concludes only exists for me in my fantasies. After a while, despite my best intentions, I am likely to start thinking in generalisations about my clients, seeing them as replicas of clients that have gone before (Hawkins & Shohet, 1990). Simply the process of translating our experience of someone else into thoughts or words can depersonalise them. RD Laing (1960) believed that no psychotherapeutic approach, no matter how humanistic or radically non-judgemental, can truly escape the distortion of the person being considered. Supervision, and indeed the process of reflective writing such as this, can free counsellors from this pattern. What happened with Alice within our three short sessions was that I lost my openness to the unique, relational encounter. And if you think people don't notice when this is happening, you're wrong.

Alice came to me via a recommendation from her health visitor, who visited her regularly due to her ill health. Despite being relatively young, in her mid-70s, Alice suffered terribly with back pain, and the poor circulation in her legs meant that getting around her home was a struggle. She also suffered crippling migraines and bouts of anxiety that meant leaving the house was difficult. She had told her health visitor that she felt very low; her health visitor arranged some counselling with me, and this was the initial presenting issue for our work together.

I visited Alice at home for our sessions. She lived alone, her husband having died quite suddenly a few years ago. She had four children: two had died in early middle age, one lived abroad and was no longer in contact with her, and the other, younger sibling lived locally but was in touch with her infrequently. She still lived in the house where she had spent all her married, family life, but the family was no longer around her. She felt, she told me, that she was struggling on with a life in which she didn't find any enjoyment.

Most of this was revealed, factually at least, in the course of our first session. Alice initially expressed very few emotions, save those that she reported upon in quite a detached way, as though it were happening to someone else: 'It is very sad to have outlived two of my children.' When I highlighted the incongruity of her experience versus the emotion that she was expressing, Alice told me, categorically, that her husband 'didn't do emotion', so neither did she. As I drove home that day, I remember reflecting that, if our sessions could allow her to safely voice emotions and memories that she'd not been allowed to express in all her married life, that might in some way be healing for Alice. Remembering my work with Bobby and Joan, this felt like a possibility.

We humans exist and come to be ourselves only in relation with others. For the philosopher Martin Buber, the problems of human existence are what develop in the intersubjective space between people, and if this is so, then healing can happen in this same space. He criticised psychologism for isolating problems within the individual psyche (Morgan-Williams, 2002). Indeed, relationships are central, even within the destructive dramas of traditional psychodynamic theory. Freud believed that socialisation is the ultimate price we pay for being human and the central problem we try to solve in the Oedipal battle (Bollas & Bonaminio, 2007). Relationships are our very existence and, thus, our interactions with each other must have the potential to heal. Therefore, the aim of therapy is to live life together and see what happens, rather than thinking of it as a place to actively solve people's problems. I wouldn't be doing this work if I didn't believe this. Yet, for some reason, I let go of this knowledge in my sessions with Alice. I began to see her as a problem to be solved, someone to be helped, rather than allowing what unfolded between us to be of itself a medium for healing. To reflect on this fully, I need first to describe the context: Alice's, mine and that of the relationship itself.

Alice's home revealed the stark differences of her past and her present. The hard and soft furnishings in the house, while clean and neat, were at least 20 or 30 years old. The kitchen bore little evidence of modern appliances but carried the scars of a busy family space inhabited by four growing children: scuff marks, scratches, the remnants of peeled-off stickers, a cork noticeboard that once contained much more than the milk delivery and dustbin collection times. Through the window looking onto the garden, I could see remnants of faded, coloured plastic poking out from a rubbish pile behind the large and well-appointed shed – the tell-tale signs of the long-ago presence of a younger generation.

Given these subtle traces of the family life the house had once contained, what was most noticeable was the lack of photographs. Alice told me subsequently that she had six grandchildren, yet only one small corner of the lounge held a few photo frames. There were two grandsons' graduation pictures and a picture of Edward, her husband, alone by a lake.

All of this I had absorbed as we moved, slowly, along the hallway from the porch, past the open kitchen door and through to come to rest in the corner of the lounge, on the threshold of the conservatory.

The view of the garden slowly revealed itself as we settled into beige, firmly upholstered chairs adjacent to each other.

'Where does it feel right to begin our session?' I asked Alice, after our initial contracting conversation.

Alice held her head in her hands: 'You are very nice to come but I just don't think I can go through any of this, it is too much for my head.'

I waited.

'I suffer terribly with migraines and today it's quite bad, you see.'

I wondered if Alice's migraine meant that the session might not be in her best interests today. 'Would you like me to come back on another day, Alice, if you are in pain?'

'No, no, you are here now so we might as well talk. It's just that I don't know what good talking will do. There is so much. I've been through so much, you see, in my life, I just don't know if we can cover it all, or if I want to.'

'We can talk about whatever feels right,' I told her. 'We don't have to cover everything, but it might help to talk about some of it. We can see how we go. Shall we just start and see what happens?'

Once we began, Alice seemed able to talk about the events of her life quite easily. However, she offered considerable resistance to any consideration of emotions, and one such moment appeared to be very significant.

'I know I have a big family. I think I always wanted one as I didn't have a big family growing up and a lot of the time it was just me,' she said at one point.

'Just you?'

'Well, my father was away with his work most of the time and my stepmother told me she didn't want to see me or hear me in the house. She really didn't like me.'

Alice's brother, John, a much-treasured relationship, was considerably older than her and left the family home to work in London after the war. Aged eight, Alice had been an evacuee, sent away alone, without her elder sibling, as he was too old. She spent much of the war on a farm in rural Devon. Shy, quiet and missing home, she described the time as 'OK' and the family as 'good people', but she yearned to be at home with her mother, whom she adored. The only time Alice saw a family member in the three years she was away was when her brother arrived one day, unannounced.

'I'll never forget what he said; it has stayed with me ever since.'

I remained silent.

'I saw him coming up the path from the road and as he came up to me, he said, "Now Alice, you must be brave, our mother has died." I daren't cry and I didn't cry because he had told me I had to be brave.'

'Did you cry when you were on your own?'

'No, I couldn't. Everyone was very nice to me, but no one spoke about it. I just got on with it. It was the war, everyone was dying, why was I any different?'

I remember thinking, already, that maybe we could give her permission to feel something now.

'You loved your mother,' I pressed gently.

'Yes.' This was said emphatically but as a matter of fact, not feelingly.

'And you felt sad when you heard that she had died.'

'Yes.' This was said questioningly, almost bitingly; why was I even asking it? 'It was a shock.'

I felt a strong sense of irritation coming from Alice, but I persisted.

'However, you weren't allowed to cry.'

A pause. A blink.

'How is it to hear me say that back to you?'

'What?' Alice frowned at me. 'I don't understand what you mean. This is all hurting my head so much, I'm not sure it's a good thing to go back over.' Here Alice closed her eyes and held her head again.

'Of course, of course. Going back over this time is hard.' I remember saying this gently, aware that this felt too much for Alice.

'Well it doesn't change anything does it? It wasn't my brother's fault he said that. He thought he was being helpful.'

I emphasised to Alice that everything we explored together was done without judgement. I also emphasised, as I always did, that these were her sessions and we would only explore what she wanted. Alice seemed calmed by this and we agreed to finish our session early, due to her headache. We agreed that she would call me next week if she was feeling unwell again.

As I reflect on this now, I realise that I was also splitting off the process of what was happening from the feeling. I did all the right things here, ethically: I gave Alice autonomy and choice and I focused on her wellbeing. Yet I realise now that, as I wrote up my reflections and approached our next session, I had already decided that I knew what would be helpful for her; I wasn't being curious and I wasn't feeling into what was happening. My reflections were cognitive and theoretical.

The road to therapeutic intimacy with a client is full of obstructions and never straightforward (Mearns & Thorne, 2000). Alice was telling me openly that her memories were painful and that thinking about them differently was hard. Yet I, head crammed with developmental theory and ideas about recreating narratives, ignored this. I acknowledged it on the surface, but not at a relational level. If we go back to Maslow's (1968) theorising on human growth and the hierarchy of needs, we learn that physiological needs and safety must be secure before we are able to satisfy our need for intimacy and emotions. Thus, it could be argued that the first hurdle for the therapeutic relationship to get over is whether our clients feel ontologically safe. If not, they are unlikely to be ready to engage in emotional explorations and it may be unethical and risky to do so. The role of a counsellor at this stage may be simply to be there. If we return to Buber, he proposes that meanings emerge when we interrelate, when we stop viewing each other as objects or, in the modern-day therapeutic equivalent, as problems to be fixed (Morgan-Williams, 2002). Existential therapist Ernesto Spinelli therefore encourages us to orientate ourselves towards our clients with 'un-knowing': that is to say, we 'attempt to remain as open as possible to whatever presents itself to our relational experience' (2013: 6). Instead, at this point with Alice, I orientated myself from a place of knowing – or believing I knew.

One of the principles of truly reflective counselling practice is the commitment to noticing when we are asking others to carry our own issues. My personal therapy over the course of my training, and since, has been a powerful place to explore the frame through which I see the world. I regard myself as a safe pair of hands, someone who gets things done, solves problems and helps others. Over the years, this has enabled me to dodge uncertainty and receive validation that I have a place in this world. I learned this at the apron strings of my generous-hearted mother, whose caring contribution to the community where we lived was consistent, loyal and considerable, and still is to this day. She developed this characteristic through her parents, who both tirelessly volunteered their time with local organisations. Ironically, it continued its development through the discourse of Thatcherite

Britain, within which I grew up, which prized individualism and independence. We children of Thatcher grew up believing in ourselves: that we could do anything we set out to do. Therefore, I have within me a heady combination of energetic helping. This, however, is my stuff; Alice should not have had to carry it for me.

I returned to Alice two weeks later, as in the morning before our next session she had called to tell me she wasn't feeling well enough. We had subsequently rescheduled but for a different day the following week, due to a doctor's appointment. When I arrived, Alice looked very surprised to see me. She eventually let me in, out of duty, I felt. She'd forgotten I was coming and I sensed that, if she had remembered, she might have cancelled again. I reminded her, still on the doorstep, that we had arranged a different day and time due to the doctor's appointment. 'Oh,' she said. We were still standing on the doorstep. Then she sighed: 'Well you'd better come in, as you've come all this way,' and she opened the door wide enough for me to enter.

This is a tricky area, ethically. When clients come to see us in our own counselling spaces, they make an active, autonomous choice to show up or not, or an involuntary omission to attend if they have forgotten. When, as in this situation, I am visiting a client in their own home and they have forgotten, it can feel as though I've ambushed them. They may not want the session but feel they are obliged to agree to it: 'You've come all this way.' The best way to address this is honestly, in the moment. If I actively address it, then it relieves any tension or resentment; my clients need not feel that they have to agree to a session just because I am standing on their doorstep.

'Alice, if you are not ready to have the session or have something else planned, that is OK with me,' I said, as we sank down into our respective chairs.

'No, no, it'll be fine. I am feeling a little down today, but I will be OK.'

'I feel like you might be saying that to be polite. Please do what is right for you.'

Alice didn't acknowledge this. Instead she told me today was not a good day. She had been in tears to the doctors already and couldn't cope.

I reflected back: 'Mmm. You don't feel you can cope today.'

'Well, I can't stop crying all the time. It starts when I get up, it makes me ill and I'm so frustrated by it.'

My theorising about Alice in the intervening couple of weeks immediately led me to wonder if a lifetime of holding back emotions was now spilling out. So here, you see, instead of staying in the moment with her lived experience, already I had moved away from her and was, frankly, objectifying her experience.

'When we met for our first session, we covered a lot of ground and you told me how overwhelming it feels. I wonder if we can take one experience at a time and look at it together and see if we can safely express what feelings you have. This way they may not be so overwhelming, eventually.'

'Hmmm.' She sounded non-committal.

'How does that sound?'

'We could try, but I'm not sure how I'll cope.'

'It doesn't feel OK to do that?'

'Well, no, you are the expert so let's try it that way.'

'OK.'

This was an important signpost, a clue, as it were, to Alice's psychological internal world, and I missed it. I was hurrying us along a route I had decided on and wasn't attending to what was happening between us in the here and now. How Alice had just responded may have been an artefact of the social world we inhabited together. What we know from extensive research into ageing is that, whether due to actual physiological barriers or imagined helplessness, often reinforced by the helping professions, we can begin to live according to a narrative of 'not being able to cope' (Slater, 1995). This results in an insidious undermining of autonomy, agency and individuality. The antidote to this, so logical and yet apparently so complicated to achieve, is to actively foster individual decision-making; to work to enable older people to continue to find choice and thence empowerment within the limits of their unique situation. As Derricourt and Miller point out: 'There is a need for greater emphasis to be placed on the process through which elderly people can speak for themselves, identify their own needs, assert their rights' (1992: 117).

If I'd been working by the phenomenological book, as it were, I might have reflected back to Alice that she was, in fact, the expert, not me. I would have asked what felt appropriate and helpful for her. However, I didn't. Propelled by my premature theorising that she needed permission to feel emotions for the many losses in her life and fuelled by my mission to uncover new, meaningful narratives,

I urged us on and missed what could have been happening right there between us. Alice was surely subjugating her rights, unable or unwilling to accept the responsibility of choice, capitulating to the superior knowledge of yet another 'expert' caregiver.

During my training, I spent some time working in a domestic abuse charity and researching and writing about victims of domestic abuse. One of the fundamental ethical considerations when working with this client group is to continuously and actively attend to the power dynamic within the relationship. Women and children who are victims of domestic abuse have often lived for a long time in an environment where their opportunities to make choices have been taken away from them. In some ways, working with people who are housebound, infirm, in ill health or dependent on helping organisations is not so different. There can be an increased reliance on others to facilitate many aspects of life, some as simple as getting out of bed or preparing food. This, in turn, can have the effect of reducing a dependent individual's perceived capacity to make decisions, take actions and even hold their own opinions. As a counsellor, I aim to inform clients without imposing my own morals, values or opinions on them. However, inevitably, therapy will always be shaped, involuntarily or otherwise, by the values of the counsellor and the wider influence of socio-political views; therefore, social analysis is vital in supervision to identify counsellor 'blind spots' (Rapp, 2000) and ensure they are not influencing the therapeutic process. This is never more important than when working with clients who are already experiencing imbalanced power dynamics or reduced autonomy.

The practice of psychotherapy is not immune to being ageist (Pilgrim, 1997). Ageism is a powerful social construct that laces itself around and within our language, laws, behaviours, health services and education systems, to name the foremost. One-to-one therapy can be a powerful antidote for that but, ironically, counselling can perpetuate it by unwittingly encouraging dependence on a helping figure with perceived psychological authority. Here, in this tiny moment between Alice and I, was an example of this happening. I struggle constantly against capitulating to the seductive call for direction and strive to ensure that clients are experiencing me as someone who listens and provides an environment that allows for autonomy and choice to flourish, even in the most difficult circumstances. In his work on care within residential settings, Brearly (1977: 14) concludes that one of the key tasks for ageing is to balance the dependence that we inevitably begin to experience with allowing ourselves to be as individual as possible. To be fair, I was trying to offer choice in my language, but perhaps still managed to convey a belief, unconscious at that time, that I knew best.

That week's session began with Alice talking about the premature death of her daughter, caused by addiction. She talked freely about the turbulent relationship they had in the last few years of her daughter's life; of the months with no contact, punctuated by crisis calls and hospital visits. She talked about how she consciously gave up fighting for her daughter when the addiction took its last, crippling hold. She got up from her chair quite suddenly and went off, slowly and wincing in pain, to another room to bring me back two photos. One was of her daughter, fresh faced, in soft focus and adorned in flowers as a bridesmaid, and the other was of her in her hospital bed, days before she died. In this one she was emaciated, covered in tubes and unconscious. The images, thrust quickly into my hands without warning, were shocking to look at alongside each other. I was angry that I hadn't had any warning, that I hadn't been asked if I'd like to see them or prepared for what was about to happen. As I write, I can see every detail of them in my minds' eye, recall the soft focus that blurred the edges of her daughter's face in the wedding photo and the gaping mouth, tube taped to its entrance, the bright lights highlighting every painful detail, in the hospital photo. I wonder, reflecting on it now, if the shock of seeing these images paralleled Alice's trauma of reliving the memories with me.

Perhaps this is what prompted Alice to bring them to me – she wanted me to share with her the uncomfortable impact of reliving the painful memories. I think I tried, clumsily, to acknowledge how it was to look at the two images side by side, and I think I encouraged Alice to try to acknowledge and quietly hold any feelings that it brought up. But perhaps the damage was already done to our therapeutic bond. The extent to which I could be a safe container for Alice's pain must have been compromised by the fact that I hadn't yet really listened to or accepted what Alice needed.

We sat together in silence for a while. Then Alice sighed and said: 'I do what I can to try and not think about these memories… I love my card-making.' She pointed to the open plastic boxes on the conservatory floor, just through the doorway, containing row after row of thin spines of cards in plastic covering. 'And my crocheting for premature babies' – here she reached down into a knitting bag next to her and pulled out a tiny, wool hat. 'And my dolls keep me busy, although I don't really have the energy for them like I used to.'

'Your dolls?'

'Yes, I have hundreds of them. Would you like to see them? We have some time left I think.'

We did indeed have 10 minutes before the end of our session, so I replied that I would be privileged to see her collection. Working in clients' homes affords a rich opportunity to be invited into aspects of their world that we wouldn't normally be able to access in such a submersive way. In particular, with clients whose worlds have contracted significantly and where their experience is limited to their home and very few other places, the importance placed on their environment and possessions can be heightened and is almost always therapeutically significant. Furniture and possessions often embody people and events from the past and have meaning and continuity that is not always obvious to an onlooker (Slater, 1995). This is in large part why I find working in clients' homes has a powerful influence on the clinical work. Objects, photographs and environments interact emotionally and psychologically. Exploring the spoken and body language gives clues to a client's worldview or psychological process and our own response can also be revealing. I once worked with someone whose wife had died on the floor of their bathroom; he wanted to take me into the room and describe the events as part of our work. My own response, repelled as I was by the cold, white space, and our exploration of how comfortable he appeared to be in there, allowed us to explore his connection to her death.

Alice led me up a narrow staircase and around the landing, past an out-dated bathroom and two simply arranged, neat bedrooms, and into the last, a box room. As I crossed the threshold, I caught my first glimpse of shelf after shelf of china dolls – hundreds, I calculated, displayed in a wood and glass unit that took up one and a half of the walls.

'Wow,' I exhaled.

'I actually made all of these,' Alice said.

Each doll had an individual face hand-painted on its china head; no two were the same. Each wore an intricate dress that had been hand-stitched. They stared out at us, askance, from their glass home, mouths slightly open. All over the floor were plastic and carboard boxes containing doll parts, materials, paints and brushes and, disturbing to see, an assortment of dismembered porcelain hands, feet and heads. My initial reaction was awe at the scale of the collection and at Alice's commitment and attention, as creator, to every tiny detail.

'Alice, this is incredible. What a lot of time and effort you have put into all of these.'

'Oh, it has kept me busy for many years, but I don't make them anymore. I have no idea at all what to do with them. They cost me hundreds and hundreds of pounds to make. I suppose I should sell them, but I have no idea how to do that and I am quite attached to them in my way.'

I resisted the urge to move into conversational talk; something about the dolls felt significant, so I kept silent, to allow space for Alice to express what she needed to say. Alice continued to tell me about them, picking up various presentation boxes and showing me the most precious dolls, the smallest, the ones she had made to mark special occasions, and those still unfinished. She told me she doubted she would finish them as she had less energy for it now and was finding things too difficult to focus on.

'So, there we are,' she said, as the tour drew to a close.

'I find myself wondering what these dolls mean to you?' I asked, eventually.

'Oh, nothing really, they are just a hobby I suppose.'

There was something chilling about the row upon row of expressionless faces in the room. And, like Alice, I struggled to find any connection or emotion with them. Should I have asked how her daughters felt about them? Did they get involved with the hobby? Had the dolls been something they'd enjoyed together? Should I have explored whether the hours and hours spent crafting these dolls had helped her through painful times or to avoid confronting painful experiences? I think I understood why Alice had brought me up there – it was a way of changing the focus of our session that felt right for her. She was, perhaps, trying to connect with me, test me perhaps – a little like the presentation of the photos. I tried to reach for what I was experiencing and, honestly, it was close to revulsion. I wondered about the experience of her own children throughout the journey of her creating the dolls. This all might have had the potential to take us somewhere therapeutically.

But with Alice, on balance, I think this moment of potential meeting came too late, in the session and in our relational journey.

As we returned downstairs and I prepared to leave, I asked Alice if I could come again the following week, same time, same day. I always do this when I am visiting clients at home. I believe confirming their ongoing consent is important, and particularly so when you are visiting someone at home, for the reasons discussed earlier.

'I'm really not sure. It is all quite overwhelming,' Alice replied.

'Would it feel OK for me to call you the day before and see how you are feeling?'

'Yes, yes, that would be best.'

It won't surprise the reader to hear that, when I called Alice the following week, she told me that she'd been giving it a lot of thought and she felt that at the moment she wasn't strong enough for counselling. 'It all feels too much, it makes my headaches worse,' she told me. As with anyone who comes to counselling, I reiterated that simply reaching out for support in the first place had shown courage and that Alice could return to counselling if she felt the time was right.

I admit, these two experiences – of the gentleman who cancelled and of Alice – plunged me into professional confusion, or even crisis, which is where we began this chapter. When my practice begins to frustrate or even disappoint me, I try to return to basics. I strip everything back to what I believe human beings are, in essence, and what can be healing to people in distress. Ultimately, after reflecting on my encounter with Alice, I was left with one feeling that bubbled to the surface to sustain me: clients know themselves, even when they feel they don't, and even when society subtly casts them as vulnerable and confused and needing guidance and instruction from 'experts'. Person-centred approaches that originate from Rogers' and Maslow's conceptualisations of humans as growth-orientated, as always having the capacity for self-actualisation, tell us to allow clients to find out for themselves and tell us where their areas for growth are. Some theorists have extended this into the concept of the Heroic Client (Duncan, Miller & Sparks, 2004) – one who can actively direct their own growth. As I've said before, I resonate more with the idea that direction towards growth is co-created within the therapeutic relationship.

I felt many things at the time of the phone call with Alice. First, I respected her autonomy and I had felt a sense of rightness that she had been able to voice her feelings and make her own informed choice.

The second feeling was guilt. I felt I had pushed too far and that I had missed what Alice was trying to communicate, and what I knew in my heart to be powerful in and of itself: that she simply needed meeting and accompanying, nothing more, and I had missed the moments where this was revealed and could have been explored. I had perhaps distorted Alice by imposing my framework of learning and theorising. The third was frustration that things hadn't been different. But isn't this the nature of a journey after all? We take wrong turns and these deviations lead to dead ends or delay our arrival at our destination, but they also expand our world a little more.

References

BACP (2018). *Ethical Framework for the Counselling Professions*. Lutterworth: BACP. www.bacp.co.uk/events-and-resources/ethics-and-standards/ethical-framework-for-the-counselling-professions (accessed 8 November 2018).

Bollas C, Bonaminio V (2007). *The Freudian Moment*. London: Karnac Books.

Brearly CP (1977). *Residential Work with the Elderly*. London: Routledge.

Cooper M (2003). *Existential Therapies*. London: Sage Publications.

Derricourt N, Miller C (1992). Empowering older people: an urgent task for community development in an ageing world. *Community Development Journal 27* (2): 117–121.

Duncan BL, Miller SD, Sparks JA (2004). *The Heroic Client: a revolutionary way to improve effectiveness through client-directed, outcome-informed therapy*. San Francisco, CA: Jossey-Bass Inc.

Hawkins P, Shohet R (1990). *Supervision in the Helping Professions*. Buckingham: Open University Press.

Laing RD (1960). *The Divided Self: an existential study in sanity and madness*. London: Tavistock Publications.

Maslow AH (1968). *Toward a Psychology of Being* (2nd ed). New York, NY: Van Nostrand Reinhold.

Mearns D, Thorne B (2000). *Person-Centred Therapy Today: new frontiers in theory and practice*. London: Sage Publications.

Morgan-Williams S (2002). All real living is meeting. In: du Plock S (ed). *Further Existential Challenges to the Psychotherapeutic Theory and Practice: papers from Existential Analysis*. London: Society for Existential Practice (pp105–123).

Murakami H (2005). *Kafka on the Shore*. London: Vintage.

Pilgrim D (1997). *Psychotherapy and Society*. London: Sage Publications.

Rapp H (2000). Working with difference. In: Lawton B, Feltham C (eds). *Taking Supervision Forward: enquiries and trends in counselling and psychotherapy*. London: Sage Publications (pp93–112).

Slater R (1995). *The Psychology of Growing Old: looking forward*. Buckingham: Open University Press.

Spinelli E (2013). *Tales of Unknowing: therapeutic encounters from an existential perspective*. Ross-on-Wye: PCCS Books.

Thanks for the fish
Cliff

'Rest you then, rest, sad eyes,
Melt not in weeping,
While she lies sleeping.'
Anonymous, 'Weep You No More Sad Fountains'

Bereavement theory teaches us that people who are isolated by loss often only need someone to visit and listen as a necessary part of the grieving process (Worden, 2009). Other people in our lives often find it hard to sit with us in our pain when we are experiencing distress as it may evoke painful memories for them or they may feel awkward and helpless. Being with someone who can bear witness to and sit with you in your pain can feel significantly healing in and of itself and help build social bonds in a world without their loved one.

It was the middle of summer when I was given Cliff's details and asked to meet him. Due to my impending holiday and our organisational policy of offering just six sessions, Cliff and I had only five weeks together. I had wondered how therapeutic this time could be for him but weighed this with the possibility that there might be no one else available to visit him for at least a month or more, due to the summer break. So I decided to meet him and have that conversation with him, within the contracting process. He could decide for himself.

Cliff was nearly 76 years old, but he looked more like 90. I had been instructed to enter his house via the unlocked back door, as he was unable to walk with ease and answering the door was challenging for him. As I walked around the back of the house on my first visit, I noticed an untidy yet obviously previously well-loved garden. In the corner, shrouded by shrubs, I could just make out a fish pond.

'Cliff?' I called out, in what I hoped was a friendly way, from the kitchen door. I walked through a tatty, old-fashioned and cluttered kitchen into a tiny hall with an ancient, brown, patterned carpet and followed the voice into the front room. Cliff was seated just next to the door. He was severely restricted in his mobility and sat, pale and hunched, in his chair. Next to him was a small hostess trolley, the top shelf of which held a glass of water, various letters and leaflets and the television remote. The bottom shelf was stacked with medication. He had a domed, furrowed forehead and was obviously severely myopic, as the glasses through which he appeared to look at me had thick, dusty lenses. His right arm was shaking and his hand was clenched in a tell-tale sign of arthritis. One of the first things he said to me was, 'Oh, don't mind my arm, they really can't tell me what is wrong with it, but it won't behave.'

Cliff had been ill for 11 years. It was hard to determine exactly what caused him to be so immobile, but he told me that his wife had been his carer until she died, six months previously. Now, he was visited by a series of carers and support agencies throughout the week. He went upstairs only once a day, using a stairlift, to go to bed. His food and medication were delivered, and a nurse visited once a month to check his blood pressure and general health. Cliff told me that there was no joy in his life, other than his sons and grandchildren. He enjoyed watching television, but only if the programme wasn't upsetting. Within half an hour on that first visit, he told me that, when something on the television upset him, he looked at the tablets on the trolley next to him and felt a strong compulsion to take them all.

It was hard not to feel overwhelmed. I have found one of the best ways of confronting the emotions that surface when I'm with a client is to talk about them. 'Cliff, I hear that your children and grandchildren bring you joy, but I also hear how sad you are that Pam isn't here anymore. You've told me that at times you want to take all of your tablets and I recognise with you that, on days when things are hard, this feels like one way that you can escape. I am conscious that we have only five weeks together and I want this space to be a useful space for you. What would you like to explore in our sessions? What would be most helpful?'

Cliff blinked at me but didn't miss a beat. He told me he just wanted to talk. He said he spoke to very few people and having one hour every week to simply talk would be very helpful.

'How would it be if, when I come each week, we just talk about whatever feels right?' I said. 'If that means we talk about Pam, then great. If that means we talk about the weather, then that's also fine.' Normally, I use part of the first session to contract with the client and check out their expectations of the therapy process. Cliff had no preconceived ideas about counselling and wasn't, in fact, expressing a specific wish to alleviate his distress. He wanted someone who came into his house and didn't leave again after five minutes having dropped off a package of pills or taken his blood pressure or performed some other task related only to his physical being.

Should we deny someone a counselling service if what they want is simply company? Are counselling and company sometimes the same thing?

Loneliness is now known to be the single most important factor in long-term health. And the association runs both ways, as poor health can also result in social isolation (Banks et al, 2008; Valtorta et al, 2016). People in poor health are more than 2.5 times more likely to report feeling lonely than those reporting good health (Office for National Statistics, 2015), and older people are much more likely to be living with poor health and restricted mobility. Feeling lonely has also been shown to increase blood pressure, elevate stress levels, weaken the immune system, and heighten feelings of depression and anxiety (Office for National Statistics, 2015). I talked with my supervisor about the goals that Cliff had identified for our work together. We both agreed that, even if all I could do was provide company for one hour a week, this in some way could be therapeutic.

The realities of working with a client in their home when they are disabled and receiving home-based care is that you are likely to experience constant interruptions from people dropping in. Rarely do carers and deliveries keep to an organised timetable; after all, the housebound patient is unlikely to be out. There were many times during the five weeks we worked together that we would hear a jolly 'Cliff?' heralding the arrival of the nurse carrying a kitbag and a syringe or the delivery of his meals on wheels. Holding boundaries, maintaining confidentiality and keeping to the flow of what is happening between counsellor and client can be a challenge under these circumstances. There were also times, as with many other clients whose houses I visit, when a member of the family, whom I knew only from the narratives Cliff and I explored together, suddenly appeared in the room. This can feel quite incongruous. On one such occasion, with another client, the daughter walked in unannounced ('So sorry, I won't be long'), made her father a cup of tea and, as she left, said to me breezily, 'Thank goodness Dad is having these sessions. Without you, he'd be dead by now!' I am not proud to admit I was left, my mouth open, in speechless shock.

Do these boundary incursions mean that we shouldn't be conducting counselling sessions in a client's home? I don't believe so. However, they need to be navigated carefully. My experiences have taught me that the contracting process needs to be ongoing and fluid. These new experiences need to be seen as an opportunity to talk about what we could do next time. It also gives us more to work with – a rich source to explore in order to get to know what life is like for that person; an invitation, if you like, into their intimate world, both interpersonally and practically.

'What is it like having people pop in at your back door unannounced?' I asked Cliff on one such occasion, once the nurse had left.

'I kind of like it,' he replied.

'You like it,' I said.

'Life can get very monotonous here on my own. And I need these people to come so I can stay here so I don't find it difficult.'

'I wonder what it would be like if we were talking about something sensitive and we were interrupted next time?'

'I think that would be OK.'

I considered asking if Cliff would like to phone the surgery and let them know what time our sessions took place. However, I reflected that this might have been more my issue than his. I had a limited time for our visits; I had to go on to another client after his session and this might have made me more impatient with our interruptions. Perhaps I also felt disempowered as I had no control over our surroundings in the way that I might if we were meeting in a counselling room of my choice, which, rightly or wrongly, gives a certain element of control and power to the counsellor (McLeod, 2013).

I understand from a theoretical standpoint that how I feel about my role in my relationships with clients is far from the most important element, and yet it has a bearing on what takes place. My emotional response was that I felt unimportant in some way – incidental. This was difficult for me to admit to myself. These considerations were helpful for me to reflect on, as they gave me a valuable lived experience of what it might be like to be Cliff in his world, where he had little personal power or autonomy or, indeed, control over who visited and when. I decided not to pursue this further: I'd checked it out with him and he felt it was OK.

My sessions with Cliff bounced between past and present, between a rich but unremarkable life story and the present torment of medication, physical limitations, medical appointments and his grief for Pam. I am strikingly aware of the amount of words and pages given over in this book to writing about and reflecting on loss. However, loss is a constant companion of the profoundly old and of those with chronic ill health; it is an inescapable fact of life for the very old. BJ Miller, a hospice carer, speaks beautifully in his TED talk (2015) about a particular client and what seems important to those approaching the end of their life: 'Most of the time we spend thinking out loud together about his life – really, about our lives. In this way, Frank grieves. In this way, he keeps up with his losses as they roll in, so that he's ready to take in the next moment.'

Older age can bring about a succession of losses: loss of working life and the identity associated with it; deaths of friends and family; reduction in physical strength; loss of personal and economic power; loss of independence; loss of health and home... the list goes on. Talking about and reflecting on life stories can help anchor our selfhood against the rising tides of change (Viney, 1993). This is what I think Cliff meant when he said he just 'wanted to talk'.

I took my seat on that first day, having (as I do always) first asked where Cliff would like me to sit, in an Ikea chair covered with a well-worn blanket, nestled in a shelved corner stuffed with books, photos, boxes, letters and ornaments of dogs. Bubbling away over my shoulder, giving off a strange blue light, was a fish tank in which a few fish silently bobbed and dived. Cliff was sitting diagonally opposite me, sunk into a vast brown sofa, flanked by his hostess trolley. Beyond his shoulder, on a corner shelf, was a black-and-white wedding photo and, next to it, a faded colour photo of the same couple, some decades later.

Sighing, Cliff began to talk: 'Do you see this [he indicated to a large mole on his left cheek]? I am going to have an operation on this next week. Cancerous they say.'

'Ah,' I replied.

Cliff slowly bent towards the letters on the trolley next him and, with his good hand, rifled painfully slowly through them to find the one he wanted, then bent over even further to offer it to me.

'See? I think it's the 24th. Anyway, they are asking for me to come in and the surgeon will take it off.'

'I'm sorry to hear you have to go through that.'

'Do you know, I was a postman for 20 years, you see. They always gave us caps to wear and actually that's the worst thing for us because our faces still used to get burnt in the sun.'

I waited.

'Hats with wide brims would have stopped that, but there you are, they didn't really care about us there; we just had to get on with it.'

He stopped here and appeared to be thinking.

'I've been going backwards and forwards to the hospital for months for them to look at my head and eyes and to take my blood as they keep telling me my arm thing is actually Parkinson's. I remember the nurse checking out my eyes and not one of them noticed the dirty great lump on my face!'

Genuinely, this is how our first session started and it formed the pattern for most of the rest of them. As in the rhythm of the Gestalt cycle, the need that is uppermost in a person's experience is in the 'figure'; it is all they can see. In this case, what was most present for Cliff was his physical illness. The theory holds that we search around for a way to fulfil or answer that need and, when it is found, the need retreats into the background again (Perls, 1969). Cliff's accounts of his life, his making contact with parts of his past experiences and emotional responses, seemed to soothe him, or at least to complete his Gestalt. So, we started with now, cycled back into the past and then returned to the now. Listening to someone talk about their past is part of how we honour them as an individual; it keeps us anchored in their idiographic experiences and away from stereotypes (Slater, 1995). It is the same for people needing to talk about death: when we are young, we can dismiss thoughts of death more easily; when death feels closer, there is an urgency to find meaning in life (Scrutton, 1999). My experience with Cliff, of his cycling between his past and the infirmity of his present, certainly bore out this pattern.

Cliff was one of four siblings, brought up by his parents in a quiet cul-de-sac a few hundred metres from where he now lived. He remembered growing up with the other children in the street, playing outside and tumbling in and out of each other's houses, never quite knowing which adult was supposed to be responsible for him at that moment in time but certain that he was safe. His mother was a seamstress, his father a mill worker. Once a year the whole family would take the train to Hastings, to stay in the caravan of a family friend and have a week's holiday. Cliff was a twin. By the age of 14, the brothers fell out regularly. He was smaller and weaker and remembers his twin brother beating him up 'because he could'. He suffered with allergies and severe childhood asthma and was kept inside at school, unable to participate in sports with his peers. His was a relatively happy childhood on balance, but he only really felt a sense of belonging and inclusion when he met Pam, a cleaner in the hardware company where he first worked.

'There she is, Pam, in that photo up on the fireplace. Look at her smile. First thing I noticed about her was her smile, so kind she was.' He pointed to a black and white photo of a lady with dark, short, permed hair, who was shyly smiling from under a hand raised to the sun.

'Shall I bring the photo over, so we can see her better?'

'Yes, bring it over.' Cliff held it in his hands and squinted through his glasses. I watched his face for emotion, checked myself for any that registered in me.

'She does look kind,' I concurred.

'Oh, she always looked after me. As I said, I was sickly growing up and when I got a bit older I was always a bit worried about things, you know? She always kept me calm and steady. Wonderful cook. We had a caravan when the boys were little, went all over in it, and she took care of us all from that little van!'

I tried to orientate myself a little better so I could look into Cliff's eyes. He was quite hunched in his seat and his eyes were angled down. He was in the room and not in the room at the same time, lost a little in the past, perhaps. In her recent novel set in a nursing home, psychiatrist Joanna Cannon's central character describes her experience of the fluidity of past and present thus: 'I looked across the lounge, and into the past. It was more useful than the present. There were times when the present felt so unimportant, so unnecessary. Just somewhere I had to dip into from time to time out of politeness' (2018: 210). My experience of working with Cliff had a similar feel: dipping into parts of the past and then snapping back into the present.

'Blast this hand! Look how it's shaking, and yet no one can tell me what's wrong with it. I have another appointment next week to go to…'

Cliff's physical experience of himself dominated and punctuated our sessions. On more than one occasion, he carefully showed me and talked through all the tablets he was taking. He read the leaflets to me and demonstrated the difficulty he had opening the boxes and blister packs. As the earlier extract illustrates, we oscillated between life story and current experience in a richly interwoven way. Theoretical and developmental approaches to working with older adults encourage us to find virtue and meaning in frailty (Karpen, 2016; Erikson, Erikson & Kivnick, 1989; Frankl, 1978). However, something about my lived experience of Cliff made me feel that frailty was one of the cornerstones of his whole life, not an artefact of his advancing years only.

When I reflect on how I felt in our sessions, it was like a container – as though, for the time we spent together, Cliff poured into me his experiences and frustrations and I held them for a while. When I think back to how he described meeting Pam, this began to have some resonance. Being supported was perhaps his currency; he himself had expressed this to me in different words right at the start, when he said he just wanted to talk.

I was acutely aware of Cliff's lack of physical agency, and this was reinforced each week as I entered the house from the rear kitchen door and walked into the lounge where he sat with his back to the door. It was further reinforced by the frequent visits from caregivers and his disorganised possessions, the plates piling in the sink and the walking frame by the back door. It gave me a sense of his vulnerability and heightened my feeling of youth and vitality in response. In supervision, I identified that I felt like I was treading carefully within the therapeutic relationship due to this. Emotional frailty doesn't naturally follow physical frailty, and vice versa, and yet I was holding him gingerly within our dyad.

At its heart, engendering client autonomy is about balancing trust and challenge appropriately (Bond, 2010), and a counsellor's role is to facilitate this. It is about adopting a stance that empowers rather than overpowers. Ultimately, the nature of the human condition is that we are all victims and perpetrators in some way (Rapp, 2000). From an existential perspective, it is about having a responsibility to our clients, but not for them; our aim is to help clients live authentically and thus heal themselves (Pollard, 2005). Never is this more important than in the context of working with those who are vulnerable, as a counsellor's own need for the client's strength and safety may lead her to want to influence or even direct them. In her paper discussing Foucault, Alisha Ali (2002) asserts that counsellors have an ethical responsibility to actively address power imbalance openly with clients.

With Cliff, I stuck with the existential counsellor's Get Out of Jail Free card – phenomenological enquiry.

'How are you finding this between us? How are we doing?'

'Um, do you mean how am I?'

'No, I suppose I mean how is it for you with me being here and coming each week?'

'Oh. Yes, it's good.'

'Hm. What does good mean?'

'I like that you listen, you are interested in my life and in Pam. I like having someone to visit that doesn't feel they *have* to be here.'

'Do you mean someone who feels they don't have to help you?'

He paused. 'Actually yes, now you say it like that. I know you can't help me with anything specific. You can't bring Pam back, you can't make me better, for example, but somehow it is helping me.'

'So, it's OK that I am not actually helping or doing anything specific that is helpful, but overall it is a helpful process.'

'Yes, although that sounds a bit confusing when you say it that way!'

This moment between us had the effect of freeing up what was happening. It is hard for me to even articulate how this happened. The best way to illustrate it is using a metaphor taken from Cliff's life. When he met Pam, he described feeling very comfortable and accepted by her family. He specifically formed a close relationship with her father. He was a man of few words, but a dependable, firm person. With him, Cliff learned to fish. At the weekends, they would leave in the darkness of dawn and spend the day at the fishing lakes, huddled quietly around their line. Cliff had fished throughout his marriage, teaching his sons in turn. He talked me through the medals and trophies in the shelves behind me and showed me on the maps where his favourite fishing spots were. What I value about working in a client's home is that possessions have meaning and constancy. They are the embodied past (Slater, 1995) and can carry therapeutic potential.

I was holding one of Cliff's more recent trophies: 'What does fishing give you?'

'Oh… peace and quiet. You don't have to worry about anyone or anything when you are out there. My father-in-law was such a quiet man, but he was a strong person and just very good to be around.'

'It's peaceful.'

'Life has got so many worries, you know. Like towards the end, before she died, Pam was still working so hard and she was having real trouble with her bosses and I felt so upset for her, but I could come to the fishing lake with my son and forget all about it for a while.'

'I wonder if it's hard for you not to be able to go as easily now?'

'My sons are really busy, but they take me sometimes. Look, that card next to you has a photo of all of us there in the spring. It was nice, but I was very cold and it was difficult under foot and I didn't want to fall. It's not the same, really.'

I asked if I could pick up the card and looked at the photo of the three generations of men gathered to fish. As I was doing this Cliff said: 'That's Pam there, in the box next to it.'

Such a seemingly incongruous sentence. Next to the card, almost level with my head, was a sturdy, sealed cardboard box, no bigger than one that might contain a mug.

'This is Pam,' I stated, pointing towards it.

'Yes. Don't really know what to do with her now. I suppose I am waiting until I die and we can be buried together.'

In reflecting on these moments together, it felt like what was being asked of me was to be steady and containing. To carry, if you like, the experience of fishing – peace, quiet, patience – into the room with me as a catalyst for talking about the more painful elements of Cliff's experience.

'It sounds like you have given that idea some thought.'

'Oh, I don't want to be here forever. I can't do anything for myself. As I said to you, sometimes I want to just take all those pills, so it is over sooner rather than later…'

People who are profoundly old or dying may find it difficult to talk about their death to others for fear of upsetting them. However, therapists are willing to go to places where others may not feel so comfortable, to listen and acknowledge rather than reassure and distract people from these thoughts. If we don't allow people to talk about death, the opportunity to confront their own mortality is lost. This commitment to exploring death with clients comes from the sure knowledge that we balance a concern for what is important for them with our own conscientious self-care.

Research has shown that a combination of personal therapy and supervision can most effectively support counsellors in order for them to continue to give the good quality of care required in the BACP ethical framework (Phillips, 2011; BACP, 2018). A study of what brings counsellors into personal therapy found that many have experienced depression, anxiety and conflict, thus demonstrating that what counsellors carry professionally will impact them personally. A personal therapist can be there to 'bear witness to the imprint' of what the client brings (Phillips, 2011: 149). I continue to have monthly personal therapy and I find that it helps me to collate experiences and reflect on them wholly, rather than purely in the context of a particular client. I have found this useful when clients have died, as I have the space to honour the grief and consider the personal impact of bearing witness to a person's intensely private experiences towards the end of life. It also allows me space to reflect on my own mortality. Supervision can help to identify emotional burnout, but personal therapy helps address its impact in order for me to be resilient enough to be effective and competent (Bond, 2010; Phillips, 2011). What I hope this means is that, in such moments, I am able to contain the imprint of another person conceptualising their death without feeling the need to console or cajole them out of it.

'What I hear is that living without Pam is hard and that sometimes it feels like you'd like to die too.'

'Yes, but I know I don't have the energy or guts to do it myself, so I just have to wait.'

'And how is it, to be waiting?'

'It's awful. I have been ill for ages and she was my carer. I was always assuming I was going to die first, although we didn't talk about it much. It's very frustrating being ill and being dependent and I suppose I was OK with dying.'

Here Cliff paused and looked around the room.

'Pam was working, she had so much energy right up until a few months before we found out she had cancer. I'd be waiting at home after work and she'd make my dinner and help me and then we'd watch some TV and go up to bed. It wasn't exciting, but it was us. Right from when I met her, she's been looking after me, and then when she needed me, I was too bloody poorly to care for her properly.'

He was shouting now; his words started tumbling out. I held still and silent, the strong presence in the half-light by the side of the lake.

'And then they took her, then they took her and when I wasn't ready too. I turned around to get my frame, to find my shoes, and Janet and the medics, they called out that they were going. I never even saw her cross the threshold for the last time. Our house! We came here the afternoon of our wedding and when she left here for the last time, I wasn't even with her. I'll never forgive Janet and I'll never forgive myself.'

Cliff took off his glasses and screwed up his eyes tight; drops of a few tiny tears squeezed out. He held his head. I stayed silent. My chest ached and I found it hard to breathe. There was a pause. I remember just taking breaths, in and out, for a while.

'I should have been there when they took her to the hospice.' He was quieter now.

I found myself saying: 'You loved her so much, Cliff.'

'I did, I do still,' he corrected.

'Do you have a sense of how you would like this to be different?'

Such a counselling term – even as I uttered it, I couldn't quite believe I was saying it. My mind raced away: he wants her here of course, what a stupid thing to say!

'I'd like her to be here,' his words overlapped my thoughts.

We sat a while, both knowing this was magical thinking but allowing his grief a bit of space.

In the silence I felt drawn to the box next to me on the shelf. 'And, of course, in some ways she is right here with you.'

'Yeah.'

'Yeah.'

One of the exceptions to strict boundaries that I have allowed myself through practising in client's homes is that, as I arrive and leave, I notice where there are small tasks and ask if I can do something to help. I consider this to be a basic human kindness, although I recognise that a lot could be made out of it in supervision. If I arrive at a house and a parcel has been left to the side of the porch, I will ask if my client would like me to bring it in. If the light changes or it begins to rain, I may ask if I should put on a light or close the window. If the client I am with has reduced mobility, I will offer to help, making this their decision rather than acting without asking. I passionately believe in client autonomy; however, I am also in these moments a human being whose default position is kindness.

The lure to help and do for others what they feel they can't is particularly compelling when visiting clients who are physically frail or limited in their movement. I believe that the urge to help should never be stronger than the urge to empower. In supervision, I try to regularly check in whether I am involuntarily filtering my experience of clients through social or cultural constructs (Hawkins & Shohet, 1990). Specifically, am I seeing helplessness and lack of power when there is, in fact, plenty of power there? Therefore, I mention this with caution, but I mention it for a reason. Sometimes small acts of kindness can be healing. If simply being in relatedness to others can be healing (Laing, 1960), then therapists acting like robots, denying instinctive human responses, are not allowing natural relatedness to happen.

I met Cliff at 10am each Friday. By the time I arrived, usually the post had been delivered. As I walked through the hall from the kitchen to meet him, I would say: 'The post is sitting on the mat, Cliff. Would you like me to bring it in for you or leave it for later?'

'Yes, thank you bring it in,' he would reply. And I would bring it to him before I sat down.

Usually, he would make a comment about it and, if a letter came from the hospital, he would open it and we might start talking about it as the start of our session. This felt right; we were walking through his experience of his life together, with the richness that might not be felt in the anonymity of the counselling room.

If I had walked through, picked up the post and given it to him, that would have been different. First, it was his property and I had no business picking it up without asking; second, I would have been acting on an assumption that he couldn't do it himself. Existential philosophy is built on the premise that life happens in the intersubjective space between two people; essentially, we are never alone and only exist in relation to others. Existential therapy builds on this premise and calls on us to confirm each other's unique presence rather than treat each other as objects. It calls on those of us that practise this way to simply be real and to acknowledge and truly see the person we are with (van Deurzen-Smith, 2012). This is what I mean by checking out the involuntary cultural filter. By asking Cliff, by making it his decision, I was engendering his autonomy and resisting making assumptions. It was a tiny gesture and moment, but to me a very important one.

And so back to the fish. One session, perhaps halfway through, we were talking about fishing and the sizes of fish Cliff had caught.

'I was really quite good, you know,' Cliff told me. 'That photo up there was about 15 years ago. I had just won an award at the local anglers' association competition for the largest fish. You can see I am struggling to hold it!'

'You always put them back, I suppose?'

'Oh yes, we never kept them. You can't, you know. Also, I like fish. I wouldn't want to kill them necessarily.'

'Hmm, you like fish,' I reflected.

'Yes, they are kind of calming, you know, the way they swim slowly and make no sound. People think fishing is boring, you know, but to me it isn't. When you are sitting there, you have nothing to think about or trouble you. After I worked at the post office and had all that stress with my boss and I was signed off work for a while, remember how I told you that the only thing that made me feel calm was my fish? You see the pond in my garden, I used to have over 20 koi carp in there at one time…'

'Ah yes, I think I noticed a pond in your garden.'

'Yes, it's in the corner. You can't see it so well as it has shrubs around it and a raised walkway. Have a look on the way out if you like. Anyway, I only have three left, but they are whoppers. I always ask people to give them some feed when they visit.'

'Is that what you'd like me to do today, perhaps?' I asked.

'There's a bowl of feed right by the back door. You could do that on the way out if you like, yes. When it's warm, I try to get out there if I can. I'm not so good when it's cold and wet.'

'How would it be to do that today? The sun is back out and it's not so cold – there's no wind. You can introduce me to the fish!'

This is what we did. We spent the last 15 minutes of our session making our way slowly through the house towards the back door. At the door, Cliff asked me to take a handful of food and he pulled his walking frame towards him and laid a fleece over his shoulders. I held open the door and he led the way in small, shuffling steps up a path to the pond I'd glimpsed on my first visit. Sure enough, sulkily gliding around within its depths were three bulging, orange-and-white carp. I handed Cliff half the food and asked him how I should do it – slowly or in one go? He showed me how to sprinkle it over the surface and we watched the fish bob soundlessly to the surface and suck the food back into the dark edges of the pool. It was one of those early summer days when it was warm enough to be outside as long as the sun was out from behind the cloud. Cliff decided to sit a while on a seat by the back door as I took my leave.

I enjoy metaphor and I find some solace in symmetry. You will know this by now, if you have read enough of this book. I am not impervious to the significance of my nourishing Cliff's treasured fish to keep them alive for him, perhaps as a metaphor or displacement for the nurturing I felt I couldn't give to him. Had I been braver, or more aware of it at the time, I might have explored this with him. What nourishment did he need?

This all feels like clever, after-the-fact analysis rather than authentic, moment-to-moment experience. They are important questions for me to consider and to be mindful of in my future work, but the fact is, I didn't explore this with him at all. I facilitated our ending, as I always do with all my clients when I can. I told him what a privilege it had been to spend this time with him each week and share his experiences, which I genuinely felt. I wished him well for the future and bade my goodbyes to the photos, trophies and the ashes of his wife. Then I made my way back through the hall to the kitchen door, took a handful of food, called out my farewell and, on my way back to my car, fed the bloody fish.

References

Ali A (2002). The convergence of Foucault and feminist psychiatry: exploring emancipatory knowledge-building. *Journal of Gender Studies, 11*(3): 233–242.

BACP (2018). *Ethical Framework for the Counselling Professions.* Lutterworth: BACP. www.bacp.co.uk/events-and-resources/ethics-and-standards/ethical-framework-for-the-counselling-professions (accessed 1 December 2018).

Banks J, Breeze E, Lessof C, Nazroo J (2008). *Living in the 21st century: older people in England. The 2006 English Longitudinal Study of Ageing: wave 3.* London: Institute for Fiscal Studies.

Bond T (2010). *Standards and Ethics for Counselling in Action* (3rd ed). London: Sage Publications.

Cannon J (2018). *Three Things About Elsie.* London: The Borough Press.

Erikson EH, Erikson JM, Kivnick HQ (1989). *Vital Involvement in Old Age.* New York, NY: WW Norton & Co.

Frankl VE (1978). *The Unheard Cry for Meaning: psychotherapy and humanism.* New York, NY: Simon & Schuster.

Hawkins P, Shohet R (1990). *Supervision in the Helping Professions.* Buckingham: Open University Press.

Karpen RR (2016). Coming to care. In: Wyatt-Brown AM, Karpen RR, Kivnick HQ. *The Big Move: life between turning points.* Bloomington, IN: Indiana University Press (pp29–39).

Laing RD (1960). *The Divided Self: an existential study in sanity and madness.* London: Tavistock Publications.

Maslow AH (1968). *Toward a Psychology of Being* (2nd ed). New York, NY: Van Nostrand Reinhold.

McLeod J (2013). *An Introduction to Counselling* (5th ed). Maidenhead: Open University Press.

Miller BJ (2015). *What Really Matters at the End of Life.* [Online.] TED2015; March. www.ted.com/talks/bj_miller_what_really_matters_at_the_end_of_life (accessed 21 March 2018).

Office for National Statistics (2015). *Measuring National Well-being: insights into loneliness, older people and well-being, 2015.* Newport: Office for National Statistics.

Perls FS (1969). *Gestalt Therapy Verbatim.* Gouldsboro, ME: The Gestalt Journal Press.

Phillips SB (2011). Up close and personal: a consideration of the role of personal therapy in the development of a psychotherapist. In: Klein RH, Bernard HS, Schermer VL (eds). *On Becoming a Psychotherapist: the personal and professional journey.* Oxford: Oxford University Press (pp144–164).

Pollard J (2005). Authenticity and inauthenticity. In: van Deurzen E, Arnold-Baker C (eds). *Existential Perspectives on Human Issues: a handbook for therapeutic practice.* Basingstoke: Palgrave Macmillan (pp171–179).

Rapp H (2000). Working with difference. In: Lawton B, Feltham C (eds). *Taking Supervision Forward: enquiries and trends in counselling and psychotherapy*. London: Sage Publications (pp93–112).

Scrutton S (1999). *Counselling Older People* (2nd ed). London: Arnold.

Slater R (1995). *The Psychology of Growing Old: looking forward*. Buckingham: Open University Press.

Valtorta NK, Kanaan M, Gilbody S, Ronzi S, Hanratty B (2016). Loneliness and social isolation as risk factors for coronary heart disease and stroke: systematic review and meta-analysis of longitudinal observational studies. *Heart 102* (13): 1009–1016.

Van Deurzen-Smith E (2012). *Existential Counselling and Psychotherapy in Practice* (3rd ed). London: Sage Publications.

Viney L (1993). *Life Stories*. Chichester: Wiley.

Worden W (2009). *Grief Counselling and Grief Therapy: a handbook for the mental health practitioner* (4th ed). Hove: Routledge.

Finding Frankl
Susan

'We must keep buggering on.' (Winston Churchill)
Martin Gilbert, *Churchill's War Leadership*

As I waited for the cast-iron gates to open, I considered the newly built cluster of town houses in front of me, each complemented by a clean, modern car nestled next to their front door. All around me were neatness, order, comfort and convenience. I swung into the spare parking space near to the number I was looking for, nervously breathing in as if to offset the size and grime of my rather 'rustic' Land Rover.

A diminutive lady popped her head out of the door before me and jauntily gave me a thumbs up, as if to say that I was parked in the right place, then beckoned me in and rapidly disappeared into the house. I edged into the hallway and found her briskly closing the kitchen door on the lower floor and ushering me up the stairs. 'Let's talk up here,' she threw over her shoulder, and led the way into an airy living room, with wooden floors, an orderly bookcase and two tight, tartan sofas, neatly stacked with cushions.

As we began to sit down, Susan sprung back up: 'Oh, I didn't offer you tea. I don't suppose you'd like a cup of tea?'

Offers of tea are an occupational hazard when visiting clients in their own homes, and one that can be loaded with meaning. If the offer becomes habitual, despite being refused each week, I always try to address the meaning of it head on. On one occasion, the client had grown up in a large, traditional Irish family. For her, offering tea and sharing a pot were culturally significant. My choice not to take tea with her each week was getting in the way of our relationship, and addressing it together was very helpful in moving us forward. However, at the first meeting, I always say no, as it can establish the work and the relationship on a 'friendly visitor' basis and this can be hard to pull away from into the phenomenological challenge of a true humanistic therapeutic interchange.

So, I declined the tea: 'No, no thank you,' and we settled into our chairs.

Susan had contacted me as, just on the cusp of an eagerly anticipated late retirement, her husband Mike had very suddenly died. She was 71, he was 73. She had tried to continue as before, quite successfully at first, but at some point, between the remembrance service and the first anniversary of his death, she had come to a grinding halt. Her strategy of keeping going, crafted and well-practised for the entirety of her life, wasn't working anymore and she felt paralysed by the weight of her loss. Everything that had felt possible before – taking care of grandchildren, paperwork, housework and errands – felt impossible. She woke each day to dread and despair. Worse, she told me, she couldn't stop crying at inopportune times. Susan didn't cry: 'One doesn't, you see,' she explained. Until now, that is.

Widowhood among women over the age of 65 is statistically very common. Reportedly, 3.64 million people in the UK aged 65+ live alone, which accounts for 32% of all people aged 65+ in the UK, and nearly 70% of these are women. Over the age of 75, this more than doubles to 75% of all people (Age UK, 2018). For someone who works therapeutically with people over the age of 75, loss and living alone are ever present in my work. Just because it is common doesn't make this life event any easier to bear.

In some ways, as it is expected to happen, the statistics only serve to reduce the uniqueness of the loss and profound life transition of becoming a widow. Within the extensive literature and research into the subject, one longitudinal study found that the loss of a spouse is a 'universally distressing experience', but the way that distress is experienced differs considerably, depending on the resources we have around us (Perrig-Chiello et al, 2016). Personality, health, social support structures, personal resilience and many other factors play a huge part in individualising the experience of widowhood. When working therapeutically with someone whose life partner has died, and not only with what is termed an 'off-time' loss (one that is earlier than might be expected), I believe we must search for and stay with what it means for that individual and not allow our exploration to be reduced to a universally received understanding of widowhood led by statistics.

I could have very easily found myself swayed by stereotypes during my work with Susan. Well-spoken, stoic, with neatly cropped hair and a wardrobe of practical clothes, she was the very picture of capability and coping. I learned in our early sessions that she had a close, supportive family and she was in very good physical health. It could have been easy for us to collude by moving quickly away from her sadness and into coping strategies and rebuilding her life. Luckily, between us and for different reasons, we allowed our sessions to take a subtly different path and one that, eventually at least, I hope was of value to Susan.

'Well, I have absolutely no idea what to expect!' she announced with some gusto as soon as we sat down for our first session, crossing her legs and placing her hands on her knees with an air of expectation. Her voice was clipped and emphatic, with a strong resonance of received pronunciation and just the slightest hint of a lisp.

I invited her to begin wherever felt right for her.

'Well, I'm 71. I was married to Mike for 44 years – we met quite late, you see, as he was married before, not happily I might add – and we have four children. Mike worked as a barrister, then a QC. He worked really hard all our married life and I brought up the children. Last year, Mike was due to retire after reducing his workload to a few days a week for a year or so. A month or so before this was supposed to happen, he was taken to hospital feeling very unwell and died of organ failure 12 hours later.'

This was all rattled off in a matter-of-fact way. Then she blinked, stopped and looked at me.

'That must have been a shock,' I said quietly, after a pause.

'Well, yes.' More blinking and then silence.

'… but I just had to get on with it – the children had lost their father, I still had my mother to look after, she died a few months ago actually, and there was a lot to be done.'

I waited. I had a feeling already that it would be very easy for us to slip into a back-and-forth dialogue of 'everyday' conversation. Our interchange in the few minutes since I had arrived at the door felt more like I was a friend coming for coffee and a catch-up. I was consciously trying to avoid filling the gaps in our conversation and wait to see what came – to allow some space and disorder, if you like, into the ordered environment I saw around me.

'There was a lot to be done.'

'Yes, well, the children were very upset, I had to tell all our friends and then there was the paperwork, so much of it! Mike handled all the paperwork about our finances and the house. I didn't even know where our wills were kept. It was overwhelming, and I knew I had to keep going and get it all done, for myself and for everyone. I was exhausted. Every night I would collapse on the sofa, so tired. There were times when I wanted to lie on the sofa all day and watch senseless movies. So unlike me.' Here she gave a quick, embarrassed laugh. 'But I just knew I couldn't do that; I had to keep going.'

With these last few words, Susan's gaze involuntarily floated over to the bookshelves where, I noticed, the books were arranged by author, in groups of 10 or more, with ornaments placed between each group. There were many shelves, made from expensive, polished wood. They seemed to have been tailor-made for the space and for people who loved books.

'Can you tell me about the books?' I said softly, trying not to intrude on her thoughts.

It is difficult to write extensively about a specific group of people without being tempted to draw out similarities and, thus, generalisations. Existential thinkers tell us that one way of ordering the uncertainty and chaos that our existence presents us with is to look for generalities and rules by which to anchor ourselves. In this way, they argue, we feel more connected to life and we can ignore the prospect of meaninglessness and death. While this rings true for me on many levels, on a professional level, at some point, we have to make some value judgements about 'what people are like' and we have to find a way of organising professional and ethical considerations to guide us in working with different presenting issues. I say all of this by way of an apology for the generalisations in the text to come.

For a war-time or post-war generation, austerity, hardship and loss were a daily possibility. As personified by Winston Churchill's quote at the start of the chapter, you were encouraged not to dwell on hardship but to keep going – 'carry on'. As I mentioned earlier, in relation to Joan, I have found, when working therapeutically with people who grew up in those times, that real emotional connection takes longer to build. A stiff upper lip means not dwelling on difficult times or acknowledging emotions. It is scary to be openly present and to bring one's own vulnerability to a meeting with a stranger (Spinelli, 2006). I frequently think about the similarities when I'm working with young adults; they often hide behind technology. How to break through? With teens and young adults, the most powerful thing that we can do as therapists is to climb into their world, ask them to show us the games they play online, and find the meaning in social media apps and behaviours so that it becomes a shared experience rather than a barrier to intimacy. In the same way, I have found one way to stay close to someone who expresses their emotions rarely or with difficulty is to track them patiently and stay with their experience.

'Ah well, I have finally got around to sorting them all out. We had so many of them and I was never going to read them all again and they were just gathering dust. So, I've kept those that have a particular meaning, but I would say I have given away hundreds, including a vast set of encyclopaedias.'

'That sounds like quite a task.'

'It was exhausting, but I wanted to do it now. I didn't want to get too old and not have the energy or capacity to do it properly. That way the children won't have to do it when I am unable. And when I must move to somewhere smaller, which will have to happen within the next few years, I want to have everything sorted out so it's not such a daunting task.'

All this talk of clearing out, downsizing, before she got too old didn't fit with the sprightly, capable, youthful woman I saw before me.

'You seem to have a lot of this thought out.'

'Hmmm.' At this, Susan looked down at her hands. A pause.

'I miss him terribly. Everything is daunting on my own. We were supposed to be doing this together.' Her face twisted into a grimace and I felt a pressure, a contracting of energy. It felt like Susan was, literally, holding herself together.

'Does it feel easier, or at least comforting, to make a start? Is that what you mean? I want to make sure I'm getting it as it is for you. I can feel with you that it is difficult.'

'No, ticking things off a list is just the only thing I know how to do. It is all I have ever done. I don't know how to grieve, that's the hard part.'

'It's hard to know how to grieve.'

'Yes.'

From this, I understood that Susan felt daunted by grieving, perhaps ill equipped to grieve even. 'Buggering on' had been how she had navigated life so far and there was some comfort in continuing that way. I also thought I was hearing that Susan needed us to go slowly and needed a way to understand how to grieve.

As a humanistic counsellor with a strong existential influence, I don't naturally incline towards psychoeducation. I tend to use theoretical models such as transactional analysis to help people understand communication with others, or grief theory to help clients normalise their grief, for example. However, I also believe in being flexible and open to doing things differently, which is what happened that day.

'Susan, I wonder if you are struggling to accept grieving because you don't know how to do it.'

'Yes, exactly.'

'And grieving is such a unique experience it is hard for anyone else to help…'

'Yes!'

'What I am wondering, and I'll be guided by you on this, is if I could talk to you about one way of thinking about grief that might be useful for you. Would that be OK?'

'Yes, OK, try me.'

At this point I began to talk about the dual process model (Stroebe & Schut, 1999), which was partly formed in reaction to the traditional grief work theories begun by Freud and, most influentially, continued by Elisabeth Kubler-Ross. These theories suggested, or have been interpreted as suggesting, that grief is a process that we must work through, stage by stage, in order to come out the other side – denial, anger, bargaining, depression and acceptance, perhaps not always in that order. Stroebe and Schut suggest that our experience of bereavement constantly oscillates between loss-oriented (focusing on the deceased and the meaning of the death) and restoration-oriented (practical tasks that need to be done to move forward following the loss) processes and activities, but that grief never completely goes away. With time, dual-process theory states, we are more able to move on with our lives, but we may always move between grief and non-grief. This is what I hoped would be helpful for Susan: understanding that it's normal to find yourself going from one side of the model to the other – to be coping and focused on tasks and making future plans *and* to find yourself sunk in the depths of grief – and that both are about grieving. The idea is to allow both to happen and to fluctuate between the two: to have balance where possible.

As I talked through this, Susan began to exhale. She nodded.

'I think I'm afraid of going to the other side of this model.'

Once again, I waited, to give space.

'I feel like I'll never be able to cope again if I let it out.'

'What is "it" I wonder?' I asked.

'Well...' A sigh escaped. 'The pain, the loss. I suppose also the anger. I have so much anger. And sadness, we were supposed to have this time together and now we don't.'

'That's a lot.'

'It feels like a lot.'

'In some ways, it feels easier for you to keep going.'

'Yes.'

One thing that stays with me powerfully from my training is that, with any client, the place to return to is the here and now, what is happening between us. It is an authentic way to build a therapeutic bond, to check out what we are experiencing and what it means. Sometimes it gives us a pause to breathe, but it can also take us much deeper.

'How was it just now to name those feelings to me?'

'It was OK.'

'OK,' I repeated.

'No, erm, I mean, it was surprisingly fine. Actually, it's quite a relief to say it! And I don't feel like I'm being weak, as you have no reason to judge me.'

This wasn't phrased as a question, but as a statement. However, I felt I wanted to emphasise it.

'No, I really am not judging you, my role here is to walk alongside you. And in walking alongside you today, I hear that you have had to endure a shock: your husband of so many years, the person you were supposed to spend your life with, has died very suddenly.'

'Mmm.'

'You now have to plan the rest of your life, and you are young, so it is a considerable time to spend alone. You miss him and part of you is angry he has gone.'

At this Susan allowed a very small nod and, I think, a tear, which she brushed away swiftly.

'I also feel that it isn't easy for you to say these things to me. You have only just met me, but my hope is that, at the very least, we can use this time together to give a little space to the other side of the model, as it were. Safely, and at your pace.'

'Yes, I see.'

'Would that be OK?'

'Yes, I think that sounds like a good idea.'

We were coming to the end of our first session and had only scratched the surface. Yet, in reflecting on it now as I write, I think we had already found a place to meet, despite the stiff upper lip, from which we would be able to work therapeutically.

People who are widowed often talk about loneliness as one of the worst aspects of bereavement. Clients say one of the loneliest aspects is having no one to chat to about day-to-day, banal events, like a blustery storm or a late postie. A family or personal milestone such as a birthday, the birth of a grandchild, a wedding, a death, can trigger a further sense of isolation – your lifetime companion is no longer there to make sense of it with. Loneliness can be a confusing experience, philosophically. The word 'lonely' is often conflated with being alone, with solitude, and yet these are very different emotional and physical states. Grieder (2002), as we explored earlier, proposes that being 'alone' is not the same as being 'lonely', as the former is stating a fact and the latter is describing an emotional state. He goes on to say that contemplative solitude can be a powerful experience when it is by choice, as it allows us to be unencumbered and reflective about our lives. It can be harder when forced upon us through circumstance.

Susan, as will be obvious by now from my account, was a lady who busied herself. The first 20 years of her married life had been spent running a busy household and bringing up their four children. The last 10 years with Mike had been spent caring for her mother, who was declining in health and had dementia and poor mobility. In the most recent years, two of her children had produced grandchildren, and she still looked after them three days a week.

'I find myself wondering when you find time for yourself in all of this,' I said during one of our sessions.

'Well, I have four days a week now when I'm not helping with my grandchildren and I try to keep those days free.'

'How are those days for you?'

'I feel, well, I'm not sure really. I need those days as I'm so tired when I'm with the children, but I feel lost. We had so many plans and now I am not sure what to do. I do online short courses, I read, but mostly I am very conscious that I am alone. Not that Mike was here much but it's not about being actually alone, it's more about it really only being me now.'

I think at this point I fell directly into what had perhaps been her trap all along – the urge to rescue Susan. I remember thinking: 'But you have grandchildren to spend time with! And I'm sure a woman with your capabilities could volunteer and spend time helping others?'

So, I said, not yet realising I was reinforcing her experience: 'What else could you spend your time doing?'

Susan paused a little here and frowned: 'Do you mean classes or volunteering?'

'I'm not sure. I wondered if we could explore what you might like to do.' I felt less sure now, wavering.

'Yes, um, I think that's my point. I feel lost, but I think part of me knows I need to be on my own, to have no one demand anything of me, even if I feel miserable. I'm just so tired – not just physically but emotionally and psychologically too. I'd like to not be needed for a while. To work out what I need.' A pause.

'Actually, that feels really rather good to admit!' she continued, with a wry smile. 'Because I can say that to you without feeling like I'm being selfish.'

And there it was. Person-centred approaches based on Rogers' and Maslow's conceptualisations of humans as perpetually growth-orientated advocate allowing clients to speak freely and to sense for themselves where their areas for growth are. The concept of the Heroic Client (Duncan, Miller & Sparks, 2004) takes this idea further by stating that, given the right conditions, a client will eventually direct her own growth. I resonate more with the idea that it is within the therapy relationship that this direction towards growth is co-created, but I fully subscribe to the idea that clients know better what works for them – of course they do. Meaning-oriented theorists argue that people are more contented when they understand what is meaningful and important to them (for example, Frankl, 1977). They go on to say that, if what people want can't be achieved, they will become distressed, and often this happens when people are in fact in opposition to themselves (Cooper,

2017). Susan seemed to be saying that she wanted to choose to be alone and, in choosing solitude, guilty though she might feel, she gained a little of herself back. She also recognised that this was counter to how she had been for most of her life: it was a struggle.

'You'd like to not be needed for a while.'

'Yes, and not to do stuff all the time but just to "be", you know?'

'I think I understand, yes. I also wonder if this is one of the first times you have let yourself think that and be OK with it.'

'Yes, yes, I think so.'

I think, socially, there is general acceptance that being alone (a statement of fact) is not a positive thing. Certainly, loneliness (an emotional state), as discussed in Cliff's chapter, can have profound effects on mental and physical health. What I've learned from Susan is that those of us working as counsellors or carers of those who are widowed and living alone should not assume that loneliness is a bad thing. It is something to be explored, to find meaning in, and perhaps to challenge. For Susan, being busy had defined her life until now, but Mike's death, devastating though it was for her, and the death of her mother some months later, had afforded her a rare opportunity to be free to choose how she did things. I was wrong to suggest she might want to find other ways to occupy her time. Solitude, when she chose it, might be a powerful antidote to her life to date and not one that she was afraid of, even though it wasn't easy for her.

It was a difficult decision to include this account of my time with Susan in the book. To my mind, she was (comparatively, given the ages of the other clients in the book) young, and much of the work between us centred on the grief of untimely widowhood. Yet, I am including it as I hope it bears witness to the importance of not being seduced by the significant power of stoicism or by the social acceptance of widowhood as something to be expected in later life and not something that could cause major grief.

I recently read Tolstoy's *The Death of Ivan Ilyich* (1886/2008), inspired to do so by other writers that I greatly value. Towards the end of his illness, as he is approaching imminent death, Ilyich becomes enraged by the way his friends, family and doctors refuse to talk to him about the fact that he is soon to die. In fact, it is this that causes most of his suffering, far worse than the physical pain he is enduring. My limited experience of working therapeutically with people who have been widowed is that it is all too evident to them that they too will die, and yet no one, least of all the bereaved family, wants to entertain any conversation about this. Yet, for a time at least, it is a starkly real consideration for the spouse left behind.

With Susan it came up in a roundabout way. One day we were talking about her relationship with her mother. She and her four siblings had been brought up in considerable wealth but with very little contact with their parents. They were cared for by staff, out of sight and out of mind. Susan was dispatched to boarding school from age nine and her earliest memories were of big parties and Christmas and other special occasions where she watched reverently as her mother blossomed into a charming, engaging hostess, nothing like the harsh, emotionless parent that Susan and her siblings experienced day to day. As her siblings were spread geographically across several countries and harboured ill feeling towards their mother, it fell to Susan, the youngest, to organise care when her mother become too poorly to care for herself. Even before dementia took its grip on her mother's personality and behaviour, she would shout at Susan, insult her, blame her for the situation she found herself in and demand Susan came to see her several times a week.

When her mother died some months after Mike, Susan experienced it as a tremendous relief. She took the decision not to attend the funeral. Her mother's illness had culminated in her making wild accusations to care home staff about Susan trying to kill her and shrieking in fear when Susan approached her, and Susan had decided not to distress her further by visiting her. She told me how she'd said her goodbye and grieved for her long before she actually died. 'One of my overriding feelings when Mike died was anger towards my mother. So much of our last few years together were dominated by her demands.' We were sitting one day, mostly in silence, after talking about her mother, allowing space for these complicated emotions to surface, and then Susan said, resolutely and emphatically: 'I will do everything in my power now to organise my life so that I am not like her.'

'To "organise your life"...?'

'Yes, well, 'Susan briskly interrupted, 'Mike did everything for us – sorted our finances and our legal documents, the mortgage, the house... I have to,' and here she faltered, as though it was the first time she had talked like this and it didn't feel authentic, 'make plans, work out where I want to live, how much money I need to live, make provisions for the children and make choices about... oh, I don't know what, but I suppose I need to state what I want to happen when I become old and infirm and when I, you know, die.'

As we grow into older age, we can experience ourselves as being victimised by our environment, our failing body, lack of economic power, loss of loved ones. One way of thinking about later life in a growth-orientated way is to commit ourselves instead to trying to transcend our immediate environment (Birren et al, 1991). Susan wanted to try to make choices and plans now that made sense to her, rather than leave this responsibility to her children. Writing under the prospect of certain, imminent death in the Nazi concentration camps of World War Two, Victor Frankl discovered that how we take up our fate gives us opportunity to find meaning and gain some freedom (Frankl, 1977). Susan was now the head of her family; it was a large family and one that she felt considerable responsibility to, but she didn't want to be a burden on them; this was clear to her.

I wondered what being like her mother would look like, were it to happen.

'She was inherently selfish. We felt such a responsibility for her happiness in the end, and this was stifling. Nothing had been thought out; we had to consider every decision for her and invariably got it wrong...' A breath. 'Hmmm...' she faded off into silence.

After a while I asked: 'What was the hmmm? It felt like you were missing something out.'

'Well, it has just hit me that I am, indeed, very like her, without realising. I am widowed, large family etc.'

'And you don't want to be.'

'I think if I didn't think about it, I might end up that way...'

'The amazing thing is that you are reflecting on it now. So you have a choice.'

At this Susan laughed impulsively: 'Except that I don't yet have the foggiest idea what I might want to plan for or be like, ha!' At this I remember she covered her mouth with her hand, a childlike gesture which seemed to signify uncertainty.

'That feels difficult for you to consider.'

'Yes, it does. Well, no, not so much difficult – more overwhelming.'

'Overwhelming.'

'Yes, yes. Really overwhelming. But I suppose I can make a start, can't I? I've got some time.'

I am always fascinated by what the great psychotherapists of our times have to say about ageing and death, and particularly what they say when they are facing it themselves. It is all very well for them, and me too here, to wax lyrical about courage and meaning-making in life's final stages, but does that change as our own death approaches? Rogers, interviewed at the milestone age of 75, said: 'I continue to live life in a variety of growing ways… for me the process of change is life. I realize that, if I were stable and steady and static, it would be a living death' (1980: 16). According to Rogers (1980), Abraham Maslow coped with his own demise by writing almost all the way up to the end, terrified that he might not have said all he had to say. Yalom, interviewed aged 86, urges us all to live differently and better right up to our death, because it is part of our life (2018).

This isn't the point where I describe how Susan went on to enrol in university or put her house on the market and bought the smallholding she'd always dreamed of owning. The shift was much more subtle than that. In reality, the counselling work I try to do, and what I believe creates lasting change for people, is to gently push against and reveal the ways of being that a person has and hold them up as if to say, 'Is this how you want things to be for you?' It is also to identify and subvert the beliefs and values that might be received subconsciously by others, whether macro-social or cultural, or by those closest to the person in their family system. For example, were Susan to say to me, 'Well I've just got to get on with things, now haven't I?', I might be tempted to say, 'Have you?' I was encouraged in my training not to ask questions; I find it hard and, as I have written these pages, I have flinched more than once at the amount of questions I recall from my work with these clients. However, I see my role in the privileged dyad of counselling as forensically exploring, with the other person, how they experience their life and what meaning this holds. Awareness brings choice and there is freedom and growth in choice.

What happened in the remaining couple of sessions we had together was that Susan began to explore the kind of life she wanted to create for the next, and perhaps final, stage of her life. She and Mike hadn't talked about retirement much, other than fleetingly, in very practical terms, such as financial provision. Mike had always worked and was still working right up to his death. They'd briefly identified that their current home, a modern development over three floors, wouldn't be their forever home, due to the stairs. There was a vacuum where their imagined future should be. So, we meandered through ideas she had for where she might live and what she might need ('Definitely a flat and somewhere near or in town where I can easily get to the shops') and what she might want to do with her time ('It would be so easy for me to consume all my time looking after my grandchildren. I need to put a limit on that and spend some time on myself').

I felt in those sessions as though my role was to hold a space for Susan to reflect and say out loud the things that were either overwhelming – she didn't want her children to have to look after her, so she wanted to identify a care home now where she would be happy – or difficult – that she was beginning to realise she was going to die alone and so wanted to challenge herself to spend more time with herself, to be better in her own company. In some ways, this appeared to be a very practical exercise, but my hope was that it also felt existential, so that, within the words that were expressed, Susan was identifying the values, beliefs and purpose of her life and was directly addressing the prospect of her own death. This was a world away from my rather clumsy question about what classes Susan might take or volunteering she might do, perhaps informed by the stereotype of an industrious widow searching for something to fill her time. With Joan, who we met earlier in the book, hers was an explicit request for help; with Susan, we'd have been doing her a disservice to march her forwards into action. Action and doing had formed so much of her life; now part of her, she recognised, simply needed time to rest and reflect.

Much of the literature about later life and ageing focuses on the loss experienced as the home environment changes, either through adaptation for mobility or through moving to sheltered accommodation or a care home setting. Rightly, the literature comments on the fact that these big adjustments are often made not through choice but necessity and can coincide with times of intense stress, such as loss of a partner or coping with illness. Writing about her own experience of 'the last big move' into assisted living following her husband's illness, Anne Wyatt-Brown (2016), in her book, *The Big Move*, suggests an alternative way of approaching this transition. Ruth Karpen, a colleague who writes alongside her in the book, reflects instead that we need to inhabit new spaces and ways of living as we age, not only physically but emotionally and existentially: that we search for meaning and reward within the changes that are imposed upon us, rather than being their victim (Karpen, 2016).

As always, as my work with Susan came to an end, I asked how it had been.

'We've been meeting together for a few months now and today is our last session together and I'm wondering how this has been for you and what it means that we are ending?'

As usual, Susan was honest and sparing with her words. 'Well, I don't feel like I have any answers yet, but I do feel so much brighter.'

'Answers?'

'I still don't really know what I'm going to do but the pain and all the crying is more bearable and is happening less and I feel I know why it is happening and can just, you know, let it happen.'

'That's good.'

'Yes.' And then Susan made a little, wry smile.

'You are smiling.'

'Well, I also feel now that I can be a bit selfish you know… think about what I want in my life, tell people what I will and won't do and take time to do stuff for me. I've earned that right, haven't I?'

'Are you asking my permission?' I laughed gently.

'Ha! No, I'm not, I know the answer to that myself.'

My hope is that we started something together that had momentum, and I said that to her as we ended our session. Things weren't 'better'; of course, they weren't: Susan was grieving for the loss of her husband and was still angry with her mother. She still had an overwhelming pile of bills and paperwork to deal with and uncertainty about the future. What we had done was understand together the meaning within all that and create a space where she could experiment with voicing how she might like her life to be and give herself permission to make choices that were for her. In many ways, this shift was revealed in a tiny moment towards the end of our work.

Susan had once told me that, for most of her life, she had been someone who got things done. This had been my first impression of her – efficient, capable, busy. As I rose to leave at the end of one of our last sessions, on a particularly dreary, wet day, Susan looked at the rain streaking down the windows and announced that all she wanted to do was curl up on the sofa and watch movies for the afternoon. She said this with a sheepish look. I remained silent, slightly raising my eyebrows. 'Oh yes… I could, couldn't I? I mean, who's to know or care?' Susan said. And she did it. For me, this was a fist-pumping moment of change. Just for a moment Susan had stopped buggering on and just was.

References

Age UK (2018). *New analysis shows number of older people with unmet care needs soars to record high.* Press release. London: Age UK. www.ageuk.org.uk/latest-press/articles/2018/july-2018/new-analysis-shows-number-of-older-people-with-unmet-care-needs-soars-to-record-high/ (accessed 8 November 2018).

Birren JE, Lubben JE, Rowe JC, Deutchman DE (1991). *The Concept and Measurement of Quality of Life in the Frail Elderly.* San Diego, CA: Academic Press.

Cooper M (2017). Synergy, dysergy and the alleviation of preventable suffering. In: Anderson RE (ed). *Alleviating World Suffering: the challenge of negative quality of life.* New York, NY: Springer (pp73–83).

Duncan BL, Miller SD, Sparks JA (2004). *The Heroic Client: a revolutionary way to improve effectiveness through client-directed, outcome-informed therapy.* San Francisco, CA: Jossey-Bass Inc.

Frankl VE (1977). *Man's Search for Meaning: an introduction to logotherapy.* New York, NY: Pocket Books.

Grieder A (2002). Solitude: a phenomenological approach. In: du Plock S (ed). *Further Existential Challenges to the Psychotherapeutic Theory and Practice: papers from Existential Analysis.* London: Society for Existential Practice (pp226–237).

Karpen RR (2016). Coming to care. In: Wyatt-Brown AM, Karpen RR, Kivnick HQ. *The Big Move: life between turning points.* Bloomington, IN: Indiana University Press (pp29–39).

Perrig-Chiello P, Spahni S, Höpflinger F, Carr D (2016). Cohort and gender differences in psychosocial adjustment to later-life widowhood. *The Journals of Gerontology: Series B 71* (4): 765–774.

Rogers CR (1980). Growing old or older and growing. *Journal of Humanistic Psychology 20* (4): 5–16.

Spinelli E (2006). *Tales of Un-knowing: therapeutic encounters from an existential perspective.* Ross-on-Wye: PCCS Books.

Stroebe MS, Schut H (1999). The dual process model of coping with bereavement: rationale and description. *Death Studies 23*(3): 197–224.

Tolstoy L (1886/2008). *The Death of Ivan Ilyich and Other Stories.* Harmondsworth: Penguin.

Wyatt-Brown AM (2016). A wife's life, a humanist's journey 2010–12. In: Wyatt-Brown AM, Karpen RR, Kivnick HQ. *The Big Move: life between turning points.* Bloomington, IN: Indiana University Press (pp9–26).

Yalom I (2018). Irvin Yalom on the possibilities of aging. [Online.] *Psychotherapy Networker*; 17 March. www.psychotherapynetworker.org/blog/details/1400/irvin-yalom-on-the-possibilities-of-aging (accessed 1 December 2018).

Waiting for the Southsea bus
Tom

'Can you imagine what your life will be like without the
protection of your Clan? You will have to hunt for yourself,
heal yourself if you get hurt. There will be no one to share your
victories. Or your defeats.'
Talltail's ears twitched. 'But I will be free.'
Erin Hunter, *Tallstar's Revenge*

I've been privileged to work with some wonderful clients who, as we've
travelled on their journey, have taught me not only about what works
and what doesn't work in the therapeutic encounter, but about life and
about my own selfhood. Sitting with a 95-year-old man exploring the
meaning of his death taught me more about life than any book ever
could. Counselling with older adults, and specifically the profoundly
old, is not only important work, it is also inspiring. As these pages have
testified, it can also be stilted, awkward at times, difficult, repetitive,
exhausting and painful, but inspiring nevertheless.

Spinelli proposes that counsellors can find their work with clients
reveals aspects of their own unknowing and becomes a vehicle for
their own change (2006: 76). I read him as telling us we are given
the clients we need. This was undoubtedly the case with Tom, whose
story closes this work. Tom was my first client ever. He was referred
to the bereavement counselling service where I worked as a volunteer
by a discerning nurse at the residential care home where he was now

living. He was struggling to adjust to life alone following the death of his wife, having been transferred to this more clinical and secure setting from the warden-supported flat that they had shared happily together. Although he appeared frail, he had a strong personality and was, in fact, in reasonably good health for his 95 years, except that he was suffering from dementia. When I got the referral, as a keen counsellor still in training, I was fearful and apprehensive. I found myself wondering how I could possibly help him.

One of my tendencies, often explored in supervision and fuelled by my studies, is my need to feel that something of value has happened between me and the client: that I can accompany them through their distress into the experience of hope. Yet, here I was, faced with a client for whom I thought no such home-baked concepts of personal choice and growth seemed possible. I also began working with Tom not long after my 40th birthday, which I had approached with trepidation; it felt to me like the unwelcome advent of my middle age and the beginning of my physical decline. Erikson ruefully defines the last life stage as one where despair is the only firm foothold to be depended on (Erikson & Erikson, 1997). However, through my work with Tom, I learned that, even in these final years of life, through the gathering fog of dementia and the anguish of isolation, determination can indeed be alive and kicking.

As I begin to write about Tom, I am aware of the risk of succumbing to the socio-cultural norm of objectifying him, of presenting this unique man as merely a representative of his age-group – as part of a 'mass of elderlies' (Erikson & Erikson, 1997: 13) – or, looked at through a Jungian frame, negating his process of individuation by participating in the mass unconscious assigning of him to the archetype of The Victim (Stein, 2005). Slater (1995) asserts that, unless we make contact individually and as equals with people who are ageing or infirm and seek to understand their personal biography and identity, we risk dehumanising them. Even if society were less generalising in its response, institutional settings tend to be reductive in their approach. In her humane exploration of pre-therapy with dementia clients, Dodds (2008) notes that institutional settings often have emotional regulation and avoidance of anxiety as their ultimate goals, making us overlook the person themselves and their individual needs and feelings.

I am also aware of the risk of slipping into some misty-eyed portrait of a cosy, comforting relationship in which Tom came to find acceptance of his current state. In truth, due to his poor hearing, hunched posture and cantankerous nature, many of our sessions had the outward appearance of irritable bickering, in spite of strong moments of connection and depth. And, to save the reader from fantasy and to avoid creating unnecessary dramatic tension that might distract from us really meeting Tom, I should reveal now that, after five awkward, stuttering sessions, I arrived to find Tom gone from his room. I was summarily and abruptly told that he had died a few days before. This is an occupational hazard, you might say, but its impact on me was profound and immediate, as I will presently explore. I was devastated.

Tom was severely stooped and unsteady on his feet, although he could walk unaided. In addition, he had poor sight and was extremely hard of hearing. Indeed, sitting hunched and asleep over the remains of his lunch, as I often found him, outwardly at least he indeed looked the archetype of an elderly, infirm, dementing man. Yet Tom had organised the rail and transport networks that moved munitions for the war effort during World War Two, which he was immensely proud of. He later established himself as what he termed a 'big boss' in the railway network industry, with thousands of people under his leadership, and held numerous non-executive directorships in the same industry in his later career. His wife, Annie, a 'remarkable woman', was a career mathematician whom he respected and adored. They had no children and were very self-contained, travelling widely. This emerged gradually in fragments throughout our conversations. I felt strongly that I needed to find this person within the archetype, so I asked more questions than I would normally, prompting his memories and connections with the past.

The environment Tom lived in was, necessarily, controlled, due to the medical and clinical needs of the residents. His advancing dementia meant Tom could not go out unaccompanied into the grounds or outside the property and was under the care of social services. He was also allowed limited personal grooming items in his room, in case he hurt himself. De Beauvoir maintained that we experience old age by internalising other people's reactions to us, which are often starkly at odds with how we feel (1972); that becoming old is, in fact, a reflection of the 'other' within us. This process felt powerfully at play with Tom; the construct of his environment predicated the image of vulnerability and dependence. Indeed, Fritz Perls, founder of Gestalt therapy, believed society itself to be a 'collective psychosis' on which we should work in therapy to locate ourselves within it or set ourselves apart from it (1969). How were we to achieve this together, I wondered?

The highly dependent and largely incapable self that was reflected back from the ecosystem of the care home setting was at odds with the decisive, independent man Tom once was and still experienced himself to be. Susan Greenfield's ground-breaking work (2008) proposes that, far from being a sealed, internal state, our identity is developed by powerful, embodied experiences through our interactions with others. She conceptualises dementia as a cycle in which confused, distressed people are treated as thus by others, which in turn causes them to behave in confused and distressed ways. Hence, their identity is slowly changed to something others expect them to be. It felt very important to me, in our time together, to acknowledge Tom's inner identity, to listen to its strong voice and for my presence and responses to directly challenge his imposed identity – the 'other inside' – that he was experiencing from all those around him. Together we would mount a quiet rebellion against the constructs that surrounded and constrained him and hopefully create the right conditions within our therapeutic relationship where he would be able to actualise growth, even at the late stage of life at which he found himself (Rogers, 1951/2003).

Elderly people in today's society are often viewed with disgust (Erikson & Erikson, 1997), feared because they represent our own ageing and death (Slater, 1995), and cared for in institutional settings, rather than within their family units as respected elders. Tom frequently referred to himself, starkly, as an animal in a cage, being thrown bits of food to keep him alive. De Beauvoir describes how society treats the elderly as a 'different species'; notably, she wrote this when she was transitioning into this generation herself (1972: 9).

Being unable to go outside of the home when he chose and on his own caused Tom great distress. This continual mismatch between his experience of himself and his experience of the situation he found himself in came up at our very first encounter and it dominated our interactions thereafter. For our first session, we settled ourselves into two chairs near the window in his room. It was March; a lukewarm breeze wandered in though the open window and a few daffodils scattered the lawn below us. Tom rotated his head towards me and peered diagonally upwards towards my face, unable to fully lift his head in my direction.

I was nervous, I had no idea what was about to happen. I was running on instinct. 'Trust your process and your training and just be here in this moment, the rest will happen,' I told myself, faithfully.

'Tom, my name is Helen. I am a counsellor. Do you know what that is?'

'A WHAT?' he shouted, squinting at me and wiping his mouth with his hanky at the same time.

'I am a counsellor. What that means is that I am here for you and you only. You can say anything to me about what's going on for you and we can see how you are feeling and why you might feel that way. I don't have to say anything about what happens between us to anyone else, or at least if I think we need to tell anyone else we will talk about it first. How it works is that I will come each week, if you want me to, for six weeks at first, and more if we think you want me to come for a little longer. How does that sound?'

Tom gave this some thought.

'Are you with that lady from social services? She's got it in for me,' he finished, dismissively.

'No, no, I'm not with social services. I volunteer with a charity that supports people whose loved ones have died. I am here because one of the nurses thought you might want to talk about how you feel since Annie died.'

At the mention of his wife's name, Tom looked directly at me, listening intently for a second. Then, after a breath, he said loudly and angrily and seemingly à propos of nothing: 'Well. I don't understand why I am in this place. Can you tell me why I am here?'

The change of subject caused me to pause briefly – had we contracted yet? I decided I had at least communicated the basics and that we could continue and come back to contracting if, and indeed when, we were able to progress. Instinctively, I returned to his question, his challenge, taking the words literally. It felt obvious to me, from my standpoint, why he was here; he was getting regular and nutritious meals and help with personal care in a warm, safe environment.

'Well, Tom, I believe you are here so that the staff can take care of you, instead of you having to live alone...'

'But I want to live alone! I hate this place. They all have it in for me. I want to go to Southsea, that's where Annie and I planned to go. How do I get there? Is there a bus?'

A pause. 'Aha!' and with this his eyebrows shot up: 'Can you help me get there?'

'Well, no, Tom, I can't help you get to Southsea.'

'Well, what's the bloody point of this whole performance then? You said you were here for me!'

Wanting to get to Southsea wasn't about actually getting to Southsea, as it turned out. I think it was essentially about having the freedom to be himself, to live in a way that made sense and, crucially, the freedom to die, alone and on his terms. I didn't yet know this; he'd have to ask me a few more times and with a bit more anger and misunderstanding before I finally figured that out.

In this moment, what I said only resulted in more frustration and anger. Nietzsche, writing about the truth within language, proposes that what a word signifies and its experienced meaning are vastly different (Harding, 2002). In his most lucid times, Tom articulated that he wanted to live in a cottage by himself and die there. I sense now that the question he posed to me about why he was there was not literal in the way that I understood it; it was the voice of his true identity speaking through his confusion: I am a strong, independent man, so why am I here? In supervision, as our work progressed, I was able to explore the generational divide we were bridging, and I was then more able to experience the world through Tom's lens, rather than mine. Perhaps the generational gap was obscuring my understanding – I am from a generation where residential care for the elderly infirm is the norm and seen as the best care option. He was not.

We got there eventually, luckily. Seen through the lens of Martin Buber, whose ideas underpin humanistic therapy, a therapeutic encounter is a point of connection between two domains of existence (Alexander & Goldenberg, 2002). Ironically, the way in which Tom's dementia presented itself afforded us an opportunity to bring our domains together in a different, unique place. Tom often talked as though he were somewhere other than in the home. Intuitively, I did not correct him or ground him in what I took to be reality; it seemed important to be fully in his reality. Once, right at the start of a session, he announced that we were in France. He wore a distant expression, as if looking at something I couldn't see. He leaned forward, conspiratorially now, with a glint in his eye. As I leaned in expectantly, mirroring his pose, he whispered slowly: 'Can you get me to the port, do you think?'

I paused for a beat, thinking I would stay with the world he was in.

'Where do you need to go, Tom?'

'Home.'

'Home,' I repeated.

'Yes, I am safe when I am home,' he told me.

The next week, after a period of silence and holding his head between his hands, Tom finally said he wanted to locate some friends in Italy so he could tread grapes.

'They are good friends of ours, they like the same things, like wine and nice food.' Here he paused; talking was often start-stop like this. His eyes stared off somewhere beyond us.

'I can't remember their names for the life of me. There is a vineyard there and I can tread the grapes. I'd love to do that now.'

'Can you tell me more about it, what would it be like?'

Tom appeared to be thinking hard about it. His head lowered as he looked at his hands. I lowered mine a little too, trying to find the same spot.

'It's warm and shady, and the grapes pop under my feet.' A pause; he ran his hand slowly over his face.

'Do you feel anything? Are you thinking anything?' I said.

'There's nothing to worry about.'

'Nothing to worry about.'

'No.'

At our third session, I found him standing, waiting patiently in the corridor for a bus to Southsea. I ducked down a little to find his eye-line.

'Hi Tom, shall we go in your room for our meeting today?'

This was the first time I arrived to find him out of his usual chair in the corner of the lounge. Tom looked at me blankly.

'It's Helen. Do you remember? I come to see you every week to talk about how you are doing?'

'Hmmm.' He paused and looked up and down the corridor: 'I need to stay here because there is a bus to Southsea today and I don't want to miss it.'

'Ah yes, that is important, but I'd love for us to be able to chat too, maybe while you are waiting.'

'I don't want to miss it.'

'How would it be if we went into your room just here and I moved our chairs nearer to the door and we leave the door open, so we can see it if it comes?'

Tom relaxed a little, nodded and we went together, slowly and haltingly, into his room.

I realise it might seem that perhaps nothing of therapeutic value was happening. I was simply visiting an elderly gentleman in a nursing home once a week. What I learned is that therapeutic shifts can be tiny, but they accumulate and make an impact, if not always in the most obvious ways. Tom was often lucid, chatty and expressive, and his fantasies were compelling. It always felt right to honour them by reflecting them back to him and staying in his context and exploring it a little. Within each of these narratives, too, Tom seemed able to recall more about his life. His socially constructed and corporeal self may have been incarcerated in the care home, but I experienced his real self as wandering wonderfully free. I felt liberated in wandering with him without specific purpose, so different from my previous, not-so-distant career in business, and different too to my natural tendency to be anchored to facts.

In her novel about Alzheimer's, *The Wilderness*, Samantha Harvey's protagonist asks angrily why he can't say things that aren't true and makes the plea that if 'there is no freedom in words and thoughts, then where is there freedom?' (2010: 217). I read this book in parallel with meeting Tom, so felt profoundly moved by this. These places and experiences that we explored together all had one thing in common: they represented Tom as having freedom, authority and experience; they felt like expressions of his true self. I believe that travelling with him inside his world allowed us to create and maintain contact, and with this our therapeutic bond slowly had the chance to grow.

At other times Tom could be very withdrawn and hard to reach; what happened between us could often feel like pre-therapy. This was quite early in my training, so I was yet to discover that there exists a theoretical frame to hang this on, but I instinctively tried to gently meet his pre-expressive and pre-verbal self and gradually allow space for his expressive self to emerge (Prouty, Portner & van Werde, 2002). In our fifth session together, there was one particularly long period of silence when I considered that he might in fact have been drifting off to sleep. He was holding his head tightly in his hands, eyes closed and frowning, and shaking it a little. To enable us to continue our contact and to communicate to him that I was alongside him, I held my own head and said, 'Tom, you are holding your head and you are frowning.'

He opened his eyes at this, found mine and announced, assertively and clearly: 'I think I need to go to hospital.'

'Are you feeling unwell? I see you are holding your head.' I continued to hold mine, mirroring his posture.

'I need to go to a hospital. One that is for what I have got. My head is hurting.'

'Would you like me to ask the doctor to come, Tom?'

He drifted again, closing his eyes from me, shaking his head.

I spoke gently and quietly: 'You are shaking your head.'

'Hmm,' Tom assented. The silence surrounded us once more.

It was, it turned out, a prescient request; the following week I arrived to find him gone.

Thus it was that these silent moments often brought about a release of something so contrastingly lucid to the confusion and quietness that preceded them that I sensed it physically. In the early sessions, with the conceit of youth, I believed that self-actualisation was not feasible at this, the last stage of Tom's life. Yet here I was experiencing the Gestaltian principle I'd read about: here perhaps was the inner self having the ability to take care of itself without outside influence. Here was confusion eventually finding its own meaning (Perls, 1969). Here, perhaps, was self-directed actualisation, even through the pain, as so extensively and eloquently proposed by Rogers (1951/2003).

Another time, Tom held his hand to his chest in perplexed silence after talking about Southsea once more and how much his wife had wanted to live there. He stopped speaking and his gaze drifted off beyond me to the floor of the room. When, at some point in the silence, I mirrored his gesture and said, 'Tom, your hand is here at your chest,' he snapped his head towards me and said in a voice raw with pain and full of vitriol: 'You cannot imagine the void I feel,' and then wept – I think, for Annie.

I tried to offer Tom my simple humanity from within his own reality and to actively resist the instinctive urge to help that was predicated by his environment, which seems to drive those working in it to minimise anxiety at all costs (Dodds, 2008). Even, for example, when he struggled to release his handkerchief from his cuff to blow his nose, I held myself until he had managed it, not rushing in to reinforce his frailty. I had witnessed, more than a few times, the absent-minded dialogue that had been co-constructed through repetition and habit among the staff of the home.

'Tom, would you like a cup of tea while your visitor is here? No? Alright there's no need to snap at me. I know you're frustrated but we are all here to help you.' 'Oh Tom, are you crying again? Don't worry, everything's going to be fine.' These are all well-meaning sentiments, but they are generic, anodyne, indiscriminate. My hope was that Tom experienced his true self with me, rather than 'the other inside', an automatic reflection of his environment and the stereotype he represented, thus in some way breaking the vicious cycle of identity change offered by Greenfield (2008).

When it is difficult to make contact, when words are not welcome or possible, it is hard to feel that anything relational is happening. These experiences with Tom, stumbling through them as I was, were a powerful lesson for me in how to simply hold the space, to communicate something even when few or no words are shared. These moments taught me that walking alongside someone in the therapeutic space means exactly that: surveying the terrain through their eyes and noticing and adopting their body positions and gestures. If we think back to how humans communicate with the very young, it is all there: we go down to their level, lie on the floor and play with them, mimic their expressions and noises back at them and what they receive is validation and reassurance of their place and safety in the world at a time when they are inherently vulnerable and unsure. The way we hold people at the very end of life may not be so different.

However, it wasn't all synchronicity; sometimes we were in outright conflict. Tom's 'void', his isolation due to 'everyone that mattered' to him having died, and his feeling that he was locked away from his previous life dominated the narrative in the sessions when we were able to have a flowing verbal dialogue. This was exacerbated by the fact that, due to his failing memory, it took time each week to re-establish contact and trust, meaning we had this conversation frequently and circuitously.

He would repeatedly say to me, almost out of the blue: 'But why you are here? What can you do for me?' I experienced this as him communicating: 'Why bother with me?' and 'You'll just let me down too,' and initially I was simply frustrated by it. I attributed his comments to an older generational critique of counselling, to a dismissal perhaps of 'all this nonsense about feelings'. Eventually, I came to see it more as an attempt to push me away in order not to disrupt his narrative of isolation.

It seemed to cause Tom further distress that his ageing experience was at odds with his own understanding of ageing, learnt from his youth and upbringing. Tom was born early in the 20th century. His mother's death affected him deeply, as did the subsequent death of his sister. He talked fondly of his mother and described in detail how she was cared for in her home and then lived with him and his wife until her death. This was the norm for that generation. Today, Tom was experiencing a different social response. According to Tom, he had no one left in the world who cared for him; he was alone. He found it difficult to remember exact details about his family members; he rarely mentioned them in our sessions and his understanding of their relationship to him varied, depending on the session and the subject matter. However, I know he had one relative, possibly a brother-in-law, and two godchildren who visited him. Yet none had offered to care for him in their home, which he found inappropriate and unusual.

I always return to Buber's theory of 'I–Thou' when I need to make sense of what happens between myself and clients. Buber suggests that, for genuine meeting of two people to take place, both 'I's must be capable of possessing a way of being in the world that allows for intersubjectivity (Alexander & Goldenberg, 2002). Initially, I feared that Tom lacked this ability. On more than one occasion I responded, perhaps defiantly, that he mattered to me: 'You keep asking me why I am here, Tom, and, as I said before, I like coming here to see you. Do you remember I told you how I work with the organisation that supports people who are grieving? I am not paid by them; I come here voluntarily because I enjoy spending time with you and it matters to me how you are feeling.'

Tom couldn't accept this. 'No, no one cares for me. You are just like the rest.'

Here I took a risk: 'You say no one cares for you but, really, do you think I care?' I tried to meet his eyes, which he had lowered to look at his hands.

Finally he conceded: 'Yes, yes I think you do… [long pause]… I like you coming anyway.'

Spinelli states that therapists offer clients both a representative of others in the world and an alternative possibility to how they are experienced (2006). The truth is that Tom mattered to me greatly and I genuinely felt compassion for him, despite his attempts to push me away with words often intended to offend. I was conscious of the power differentials within the setting, of me being free to come and go and of Tom's comparative lack of freedom. I was also acutely aware of the point of view that meaningful, emancipatory therapy is impossible, or at least difficult, in an institutional care context (McLeod, 2013). Therefore, we discussed my return each week as a process of ongoing informed consent and of allowing autonomy within the constrictions of his life. While Tom emphatically pushed me away with words, he always consented to my return. Furthermore, he would accompany me to the door when I left and, even though he did not recognise me the following week, was often wandering the corridor near the lift at the time of my visits. I took these small gestures as evidence that we were getting somewhere in building our relationship: that while he shouted at me and pushed me away, in some way he welcomed my visits.

Tom's room was devoid of photos and he had few personal possessions. Many people at the very end of life voluntarily reduce their freedom and possessions (Slater, 1995), but this felt like part of a wider process. When I asked if there were any photos Tom wanted to share with me in our sessions or searched the room for clues of his earlier life, there were simply none. In fact, Tom responded derisively: 'I hate photos that look at the past. It is gone, done. Anyway, they are too painful to see.' This last sentence was said with an air of finality. This subject was over.

Now that I have more experience of working in similar settings and with clients of Tom's age, I realise how rare this is. Often, looking at photos, letters and objects from the past brings comfort, memories and an engagement with the life that has been lived. Shorter-term memories are harder to retain; those that are longer term are more vivid and secure. Age Concern talks of overcoming pessimism as one goal of counselling older clients (Scrutton, 1999), and yet this pessimism seemed important in identifying the meaning of Tom's isolation and it felt necessary to stay with it, rather than jolly him along. I was being told that he needed no one, but something about this didn't feel authentic; it felt forced. Inspired by existential ideas, I found in it a possibility to explore the differences between his worldview narrative and what I experienced and noticed in the room during our sessions (Mearns & Cooper, 2005; van Deurzen, 2002).

During one session, I noticed a greetings card that was new on his chest of drawers. It stood out, as there were so few sentimental objects around the room. When I pointed it out, Tom told me it was from a couple who used to work for him. He dismissed them as only wanting to get their hands on the cottage he owned; he was angry with them and didn't want to talk about them further. I asked gently who else visited him. He mentioned his brother-in-law, his only surviving relative, sometimes called Peter and sometimes Roger, depending on the session, and sometimes he was his nephew instead. While the details weren't clear, the meaning of this person was vivid. This man, whoever he was, appeared to have power of attorney over Tom's affairs and Tom cast him in the role of a dark villain with ulterior motives. He fantasised readily that Peter/Roger was sending his money abroad and called him a powerful, hateful man with no interest in anyone but himself. On more than one occasion, I felt myself wanting to challenge the validity of this, but held myself back. I also felt compelled to ask the clinical lead of the care home about his family. I told myself this was to establish a picture of his support network. I realised over time that I had been drawn into the drama and I wanted to establish facts, without realising the facts were irrelevant; the meaning was everything.

When I reflected on it between sessions, Tom's account of this figure in his life evoked in me the sense of the Jungian shadow (Stein, 2005), or a retroflection from a Gestalt frame (Clarkson, 1989). I wondered whether, in the process of reflecting on his life, Tom might have been projecting his own, shameful, unlovable side onto this man.

He said to me once, quite menacingly, with a sneer: 'You can't image how despicable this man is.'

'He's despicable?' I asked.

'He is only interested in himself, he doesn't care about me or anyone else.' Tom could not entertain the notion that this man, who was looking after his affairs, had his best interests at heart. I found in this a reflection of my own experience of not being allowed to care for him, whatever my motives.

I am not so naïve that I can't recognise the symptoms of Tom's progressing dementia in this account: his bursts of anger, moments of confusion and difficulty communicating; the periods of withdrawal and silence and paranoid feelings towards others, to name a few. However, dementia is a group of diseases that affect the brain; it is a medical diagnosis; it is not an identity in itself and, while there are care pathways for dementia, what we now know for sure is that the people around someone with dementia, the relationships they have with them and the environment they exist within, can have a powerfully positive effect on that individual's experience (Alzheimer's Society, 2018). Top of the list of things that can help individuals live well with the disease are cognitive stimulation and reliving life stories (Alzheimer's Society, 2018). I was unaware of most of this when I was working with Tom; I had yet to have any training in dementia. Yet I feel my relative ignorance helped me see what happened between us as expressions of Tom's individual experience and of our therapeutic work, rather than homogenised symptoms of a disease.

If we return to Tom's insistence of his isolation, I experienced his narrative about his unloved state as a defence mechanism. Possibly I felt it more keenly as I am someone who loves and accepts love readily and openly. In reflecting on this again as I write, I wonder if the void he had expressed so viscerally after losing his wife meant that to be the 'I' within a 'Thou', as described by Buber (Harding, 2002), with anyone was a risk he couldn't take. Erikson's theory is that the life stage we have not resolved is lived out in our last stage (Erikson & Erikson, 1997) and de Beauvoir asserts that we revive unpleasant memories in later life (1972). I have found myself wondering how Tom had experienced trust in his earliest, formative relationships. This wasn't something we had explored specifically in our sessions, but I had an innate sense when in the room with him that Tom's keeping me away was a long-held, well-practised art. Of course, we didn't have the luxury of time within which to explore this in the end, so these musings only exist in my head.

My supervisor noted that I talked of loving Tom and that I had not mentioned loving any other clients, and she said that even she had come to care for him through our supervision sessions. I initially attributed this strength of feeling to some uniqueness in our work, puffed up as I was by the keenness of being a trainee, or to my need to fill his void due to an over-inflated sense of my own importance in his life. I sense now that it was far simpler than that. Tom reported that no one cared for him in the home, that his possessions went missing and that 'they' (there was always a 'they', and always uttered with the slight narrowing of his eyes) were only in it for the money. As I mentioned, according to him, I was wasting my time and initially he assumed I was only there because I was being paid. His only living relative was conceptualised as a villainous money-grabber and the nameless couple who visited him only wanted his cottage. I wondered what I was experiencing about Tom that others might have experienced too. Despite Tom's dialogue about not needing others, what registered powerfully within me was love, perhaps because what was being asked for was love. It put me in mind of Maslow's (1968) proposal that our inner nature will be heard, even if it whispers, and that our sickness only comes when we suppress something. Therapists are encouraged to meet clients at depth by responding to their defences with patience and persistence (Mearns & Cooper, 2005) and, while there was no explicit response to my loving him and persisting in my care for him, in the end there seemed to be some therapeutic shift.

In our penultimate session I noticed a bottle of wine on the bedside table. Remembering our journey together through his fantasy of treading grapes, I asked where the wine had come from: 'Two young people brought it,' he replied.

'Ah. Do you know who they were?' I asked.

Tom paused for a long time here, thinking: 'Yes, yes, they are my godchildren.'

Here he smiled, the first and one of the very few times I saw him smile, as he thought about them, and he continued eagerly to tell me he was planning to leave them his estate when he died. When he finally found their names in the fog of his memory, he said both of them out loud. Then he almost shouted: 'I remember now! I remember that they call me Uncle Tom.'

Then he wept openly and silently.

'They love you,' I said, and this time he permitted himself a small nod of assent.

My supervisor suggested to me that, by enabling Tom to experience my care and to re-experience the love of his godchildren, his anger at his isolation, which had afforded him so much fight and vitality, was subjugated and this allowed him to die. It was tempting to tie up our time together in that neat package. However, that wasn't my experience of what happened. What I think was happening between us was that Tom experienced something a little different to the prevailing attitude towards the elderly infirm; within a residential setting that permitted him no agency, he was seen as, at best, dependent, and at worst, irrelevant. His liberty, schedule and personal care were all out of his hands. And yet he was still a man of inherent agency; he was, despite his confusion, still vehemently authentic in refusing to hide himself from himself or others (van Deurzen, 2002); a man whose refusal to abide by social niceties and whose strong desire to be wandering free dominated our dialogues; a man who corrected and disputed with me and vehemently rejected platitudes and my eager suggestions that looking at some photos or listening to the radio might be of comfort. To him, the rest of the world was engaged in the lazy chatter of inauthenticity (van Deurzen, 2002), while he wanted independence and welcomed the final void of death. I like to think, albeit in my naivety and ignorance of diagnostic symptoms, that is the man I responded to in our sessions.

Tom talked often of 'clearing off', by which, we established, he meant dying. Existentialists maintain that acknowledging the ultimate ending that is death can allow us to find meaning in our life (Spinelli, 2006; Cooper, 2003). Tom had already accepted and was welcoming his own death; his anxiety came not from the event itself but from his lack of agency in it.

'You want to die.'

'Yes!' [vehemently]. 'But not here, I want to go to a little cottage somewhere and lie down on my own and not get up again.'

I stayed silent; I felt there was more to come.

'But I can't bloody leave here can I? Not even you can get me out, can you? So how can I do that?'

'It feels really difficult for you as you can't look forward to the death you would like to have, like you don't have a say in it.'

'Yes, well I could try and do it. I often lie here planning how I could do it. I could hang myself from that door there.' He pointed at the door of his room. 'But I know I don't have the strength to climb up and do it.'

Tom's chin, bristled with white, was thrust upwards a little at this, defiantly. I felt he was waiting for me to say something. What? To tell him not to be silly, to urgently call a member of staff to say that he was suicidal? I didn't do either of these; we both knew he hadn't the physical capability to end his life, nor the means, but this discussion felt like one he wanted to have.

'What else?' I asked.

'Well, I did think about cutting my wrists, but I have no razors. They have taken them from me. All I have in here is a soft brush, some soap, towels and tissues. Can't do much with them, can I?'

'So, in your cottage, what would it be like then?'

'Well I would just be very tired and I would lie down in a bed, none of these people would be there, and I would just go to sleep and that would be that.'

'That would be that.'

'Yes.'

Our first sessions were spent at a presentational level, to borrow a concept from Mearns and Cooper (2005); I naively assumed that I should keep things light and avoid distress. My sense is that once I braved a more existential standpoint and began challenging his inconsistencies, meeting his fantasies about dying head on and recognising his agency, we were finally able to meet each other.

Sartre believed we are always free and should trust our own choices (2003), yet I struggled initially to see how Tom had any freedom, bound as I was in my literal interpretation of his world. My journal from this time documents my surprise that this talk of death was not as difficult for me as I had expected. I have explored in therapy my feelings about my own death and the deaths of those I love, and it has always filled me with fear. Twelve years ago, one of the twins I was carrying died half way through my pregnancy and this loss affected me profoundly, leaving me anxious about others around me dying and raising more questions than I yet have answers for about spirituality and the after-life. I consider my own death with detached interest, as one does a final chapter in a work of fiction. I walk around it and consider it from afar, rather than engaging with it directly. However, something about Tom's need to have ownership and authorship of his death and my fierce commitment not to rescue or pity him co-created in the space between us a challenging, no-limits dialogue that naturally gave permission for this talk of death.

In Albert Camus' existential novel L'Etranger (1942/2010), Meursault considers death while awaiting his sentencing in court, having been tried for murder. He muses that being shot down suddenly while freely wandering the streets would be a simple, welcome luxury in comparison with the absolute certainty of being sentenced to death. I sensed the same feeling in Tom. My fantasy is that our work together allowed him to find some freedom, but not in the literal way I had conceptualised initially. I imagined him living out his final days in fields of vines in Italy or sitting in the faded lounge of an antediluvian hotel in Southsea, looking out to sea. Or living alone in the simple cottage, cold and remote, that he had imagined escaping to so he could die.

He died after a short time in hospital, not in the cottage that he'd passionately envisaged but at least not in the care home where he felt so confined. His death affects me deeply, still. His gift to me was a lesson in how to be with someone in despair without needing to help; how to sit patiently with silence and confusion, and how to talk about death frankly and honestly. I was angry with him for leaving me, but I was jubilant for him that he was finally free.

References

Alexander Z, Goldenberg H (2002). Between persons: the narrow ridge where I and Thou meet. In: du Plock S (ed). *Further Existential Challenges to the Psychotherapeutic Theory and Practice: papers from Existential Analysis*. London: Society for Existential Practice (pp154–165).

Alzheimer's Society (undated). *Alzheimer's Society's view on people with dementia living alone.* [Online.] London: Alzheimer's Society. https://www.alzheimers.org.uk/about-us/policy-and-influencing/what-we-think/dementia-living-alone (accessed 1 December 2018).

Alzheimer's Society (undated). *Five things you should know about dementia.* [Online.] London: Alzheimer's Society. www.alzheimers.org.uk/about-dementia/five-things-you-should-know-about-dementia (accessed 1 December 2018).

Camus A (1942/2010). *The Outsider.* London: Hamish Hamilton.

Clarkson P (1989). *Gestalt Counselling in Action.* London: Sage Publications.

Cooper M (2003). *Existential Therapies.* London: Sage Publications.

De Beauvoir S (1972). *Old Age* (P O'Brien trans). London: HarperCollins.

Dodds P (2008). *Pre-therapy and Dementia: an action research project.* Doctoral thesis. Brighton: University of Brighton.

Erikson JM, Erikson EH (1997). *The Life Cycle Completed: a review.* New York, NY: WW Norton & Company.

Greenfield S (2008). *ID: the quest for meaning in the 21st century.* London: Hodder & Stoughton.

Harding M (2002). Using language. In: du Plock S (ed). *Further Existential Challenges to the Psychotherapeutic Theory and Practice: papers from Existential Analysis.* London: Society for Existential Practice (pp339–355).

Harvey S (2010). *The Wilderness: a novel*. New York, NY: Anchor Books.

Hunter E (2014). *Warriors Super Edition: Tallstar's revenge*. London: HarperCollins.

Maslow AH (1968). *Toward a Psychology of Being* (2nd ed). New York, NY: Van Nostrand Reinhold.

McLeod J (2013). *An Introduction to Counselling* (5th ed). Maidenhead: Open University Press.

Mearns D, Cooper M (2005). *Working at Relational Depth in Counselling and Psychotherapy*. London: Sage Publications.

Perls FS (1969). *Gestalt Therapy Verbatim*. Gouldsboro, ME: The Gestalt Journal Press.

Prouty GF, Portner M, van Werde D (2002). *Pre-therapy: reaching contact impaired clients*. Ross-on-Wye: PCCS Books.

Rogers CR (1951/2003). *Client-Centred Therapy*. London: Constable.

Sartre J-P (1943/2003). *Being and Nothingness: an essay on phenomenological ontology*. London: Routledge.

Scrutton S (1999). *Counselling Older People: a creative response to ageing* (2nd ed). London: Hodder education.

Slater R (1995). *The Psychology of Growing Old: looking forward*. Buckingham: Open University Press.

Spinelli E (2006). *Tales of Un-knowing: therapeutic encounters from an existential perspective*. Ross-on-Wye: PCCS Books.

Stein M (2005). Individuation: inner work. *Journal of Jungian Theory and Practice 7*(2): 1–13.

Van Deurzen E (2002). Heidegger's challenge of authenticity. In: du Plock S (ed). *Further Existential Challenges to the Psychotherapeutic Theory and Practice: papers from Existential Analysis*. London: Society for Existential Practice (pp370–379).

Conclusion

As we reach the conclusion of this book, I want to be very clear on one important philosophical point: I am not suggesting that poor mental health or emotional distress is to be expected as we progress into our late 70s, 80s and beyond. In fact, I believe the opposite: that this increasingly lengthening period of our lives can bring choice, growth and, ultimately, peace, and in a way that other phases of life don't always allow. What I hope this book addresses is how to respond to people at various stages within this huge age group in a way that is not only ethically appropriate but also transcends social, cultural and physical limitations and stereotypes. I am seeking to raise an awareness of some of these factors that need to be held, but held lightly and appropriately, in our work. I am advocating that, when we come to our meetings with older adults in the therapeutic space, we are free of prejudice, focused on empowerment and allow for the same growth-orientated curiosity and enquiry and powerful moments of interrelating that we would hope to co-create with anyone of any age who chooses to come to counselling.

Recognition that we need to adopt an empowered, unboundaried approach to our own advancing age is quickly growing and yet it continues to meet considerable opposition in the way our legal, social and care frameworks (largely based on outdated research and theory) are structured. One of the most comprehensive longitudinal studies on happiness and ageing, conducted by Laura Carstensen (2011), shows just how much we have been socially programmed to think about the main task of ageing as 'coping', which is inherently a passive, defensive position to find ourselves in. She argues that, to enjoy the gift of longer life that we have been given by evolutionary, medical and social factors, we must age in a deliberate way that celebrates our choices. In support of this, neuropsychologist Dr Mario Martinez, who interviewed hundreds of centenarians for his research on biocognition, suggests that ageing is merely our embodied response to cultural limitations: what he calls 'cultural editors'. He suggests that we should view 'growing older' as the passage of our mind and body through space and argues that this is a process we can energetically engage with, rather than be at the mercy of (Martinez, 2016).

Counsellors are invited into other people's worlds for a brief time. I am fully aware that what can feel tolerable in that short period within the therapeutic relationship may feel heavy and distressing when it is carried over months and years. During the writing of this book, my father-in-law, a man I have known for more than 25 years and who has played an important role in the lives of my husband and children, as well as my own, was diagnosed with a grade 4 glioblastoma, the most aggressive form of brain cancer. Being with him over these months, seeing him frightened, confused and physically reduced, has profoundly affected me, emotionally and physically. Issues I may be able to hold, experience and explore with clients who are elderly or dying are immeasurably harder with someone I love.

I don't profess to be an authority on counselling older-aged clients. My aim has been only to offer a reflective account of my experiences to date in this field, in the hope that it will provoke some response in those who choose to read them. What can we, as professionals, clinicians or family and friends of those approaching older age learn from these experiences? Woven throughout these accounts are some themes that I'd like to draw out in this concluding chapter, as much for my own benefit, as I walk this journey with my family, as for the benefit of others who might read them.

Don't view people through a medical model

In Chapter 4 we met Kate, whose intersubjective experience of the world had always been filtered through the lenses of medical professionals. With Cliff, too, and his endless packets of pills and visiting health professionals, it was hard to transcend the construct of the necessary medical structure that supported him to live independently. I fed the fish, literally and metaphorically, and that was, I believe, the right, ethical decision in relation to both these clients.

But I absolutely believe that an individual's lived experience of their illness or bodily condition can exist independently of what medicine states about it, even though we may rely on medicine for curative or palliative support. What I have learned in my work so far is to continually ground myself in the phenomenological basis of my training. Ask what that individual's embodied and emotional experience is in the moment you encounter it. 'I hear that you are experiencing chronic arthritis in your joints, and I'm wondering what this feels like in your body as we sit here.' This approach allows an idiographic meaning to be formed about what is happening. Within the therapeutic space, we can be the exception to generalities, to lists of symptoms and side effects and to prognoses. All these can be helpful as a framework to understand illness, but they can also stop us from seeing the unique person in the room; walking our distinct, counselling journey alongside our client allows us uniquely to explore their psychological landscape and individual meaning.

In an academic paper written following her husband's early onset of dementia, Gaynor MacDonald (2017: 5) proposes that medicine is non-relational in its understanding of life. 'The first information a patient of a family member will be given is a rundown of the disease, its various types, its causes and the sad news that it is – at present – incurable… A diagnosis produces grief, unlike death, the person with dementia is alive and yet spoken of as lost to life'. She talks about how her husband's behavioural symptoms of dementia were actively alleviated through personal interaction. The same can be said of age-related behaviours and psychological traits. Seen through purely medical eyes, and with the certainty of degeneration and death not so far away, the agency and idiosyncrasies of the person themselves can get pushed aside and forgotten. Our job is to locate them, explore them and amplify them by connecting deeply with our clients on a personal level.

Talk about death

In his TED talk on working with people at the end of life, hospice and palliative care medical specialist BJ Miller says: 'Maybe we can learn to live well – not in spite of death, but because of it. Let death be what takes us, not lack of imagination' (Miller, 2015).

As I explored earlier in this book, various research has shown, simply, that when people who are close to death are actively encouraged to talk about it, they live longer (Gawande, 2015). But talking about death requires us to admit to ourselves that all life will end. It means we must face our own death, and that is hard. There is also an assumption that talking about death will be painful for the ageing or dying person. There is also an instinct to protect others from the knowledge that we are dying, in order not to drag them down.

However, the basis of existential therapy, in which I believe, is to find meaning and allow each of us to become who we are in our lives, in full awareness that we will one day die (van Deurzen, 2002). We all have to face our own death all of the time. It is not just the preserve of people over a certain age; our ultimate death is ever present for each of us from the moment we are born. And this belief is not just the preserve of the existentialists either. Jung argued fervently for accepting the birth of death as we approach the latter half of life, in the same way that we accept birth itself: 'The birth of a human being is pregnant with meaning, why not death? For 20 years and more the growing man is being prepared for the complete unfolding of his individual nature, why should not the older man prepare himself 20 years or more for his death?' (Jung, 1934/2014).

I am not suggesting we launch uninvited into a discussion about mortality with our clients. In my experience, acceptance and exploration of death can be held gently and navigated by tracking and reflecting the individual's lived experiences. Tom, in the last chapter in this book, wanted to die. He welcomed death as a release and he wanted to talk about the ways in which he wished to die. I responded by acknowledging and honouring this and by closely following his narrative, rather than dismissing or diminishing his feelings as taboo. When Maggie, in Chapter 1, exclaimed to me, 'Oh, I am 80. I am so old!', I resisted making assumptions about what she meant, and I resisted, too, jollying her along with a platitude. Instead we explored what it meant for her to be old and her strengthening connection to her parents as she considered her own death.

Believe in growth and change at any stage of life

Remember my chance encounter with the ladies on the train? Their sentiments were that retirement is the start of a new phase of growth. 'If

I were stable and static, I would be living death,' said Rogers in a paper written late in his own life (1980). I believe that all psychotherapists, regardless of our modality, and perhaps carers, clinicians and anyone working in the helping professions in general, hold a commitment at the core of our work to create something new for the people we work with. This should be the case for the client who is housebound, whose health is failing, whose economic power is reduced, just as it is for an adolescent who is forming their identity or a young adult with many more years, choices and opportunities ahead of them. It is our responsibility to explore what clients would like to be different in their lives and to believe that they can achieve this. As van Deurzen writes (2002), true psychotherapy is not oriented towards the actuality of our clients but to their potentiality.

Harvard-based psychologist Dan Gilbert conducted some research into how much change people expected to experience in their lives compared with how much they subsequently experienced (Gilbert, 2014). What he found was that the rate of change does slow as we age, but not as much as we think, and that, at every age, we underestimate how much our values, personalities and situation will change in the next decade. This is compelling knowledge.

Bobby, in Chapter 2, was ready to redefine who he was in the wake of the death of his wife. It was painful and awkward at times, but by staying close to my lived experience of him in the room, noticing and honouring parts of him that seemed to want to come forward, I was able to stumble with him, relationally, to find a different version of himself that he could bear. By contrast, and for different reasons, Alice and Kate found it very difficult to construct new narratives of their past from which to move forward through the next part of their lives. One of the enduring and very few factors that contribute to the success of counselling across all modalities is client involvement and engagement in growth and change (Bohart & Tallman, 2010). What the counsellor does is maintain a belief in the positive potential of the client, listen, and hold the space while they find the areas for growth themselves, as I was able to do with Bobby.

Another aspect is a commitment to explore with clients how their relationship with time, spaces, places, people and objects is changing. In the plethora of literature on the effects of ageing is an expectation that, due to changing personal and family circumstances and physical and financial limitations, one of the norms of approaching old age is that our environments can change (Wyatt-Brown, Ray & Kivnick, 2017). This may be a move to new, possibly supported accommodation or the adaption of our existing homes to meet needs such as reduced mobility. We might find ourselves no longer able to drive or unable to access places we used to inhabit, such as golf clubs or having a coffee out with friends. We do not have to be victims of this process, and we can still find powerful meaning in the environmental changes that happen as we age (Birren et al, 1991). If we return to my father-in-law, 'tinkering' with car engines in his garage has been a source of pleasure throughout his life – a pastime, if you like. In his enforced retirement and facing the prospect of dying within a matter of years, this space he has carved out for himself now provides both comfort and a legacy. Its meaning has changed, his relationship with pottering has intensified, its role in his life is now much more than a pastime. These shifting relationships can hold meaning and their exploration can be a subject for powerful reflection and a source of new choices.

Find virtue and meaning in frailty

It can be hard as a caregiver, family member or professional to transcend the visible signs of frailty when we see them in others. It is difficult not to subconsciously assume the role of a rescuer when someone appears to be struggling, either physically or emotionally. The nature of the human condition, seen through an existentialist frame, is suffering. Just as we are born knowing we will one day die, we are also inescapably always in relation to others, even in solitude, and we are bound to find meaning and live by choices that we are all free to make (Sartre, 1943/2003). Even Carl Rogers, usually known for his rather positive view of life, suggested in his paper on ageing that confusion, fear and uncertainty are the price we pay for living (Rogers, 1980). Therefore, we are all, at one point or another, suffering. This makes us all, indirectly, by turn, perpetrators and victims of suffering, even if we are not willingly so. The world is symbiotic; one person's vulnerability is counterbalanced by another's capacity for strength. As in any therapeutic dyad, we should pay attention to the pull to rescue those who appear to be more in need than us, for this of course is an illusion. We are all in need. We all close the door on our counselling room and confront the realities of our own life – a poorly relative, a challenging child, a marriage in trouble – crossing the boundary from

'I'm OK' to 'I'm not OK' in the blink of an eye. I encourage each of us to hold this awareness in our work with any person who appears vulnerable.

With Joan, in Chapter 3, for example, the physical limitations left by her stroke were frustrating for her; indeed, this was the focus of much of our sessions, but not in the way I expected. When I asked her, right at the start, if she wanted me to ring the bell when I arrived and wait for her to answer or to knock and enter so she didn't have to struggle to get up, she was indignant: getting up to greet a visitor was part of life and she wasn't about to stop doing it. However, when we talked at the end of our time together about new things she might want to start doing, we arrived at her decision to give up knitting, as she had lost the ability in one hand to grip a needle, and to try watercolour painting instead – a new group was starting up in the village. Her physical limitations brought meaning and new choices beyond simply the frustration. We need to be people who value our clients' frailty and help them explore it and perhaps depart from the norm of their experience.

One other thing to bear in mind with people with chronic conditions or taking medication is to actively explore, if this is possible, the likely impact on the work together. With Maggie, we discussed and agreed sessions of 30 minutes, as her concentration and energy only allowed for this. Her speech was also slow, so our pace slowed too, and we discussed how she felt when others finished her words for her. We agreed she would ask me for help if she wanted it. With Kate, when it became evident that she was taking Lorazepam, we used this moment to explore the other medication she was on and the likely effects on our work. One was that she became tired at certain points of the day (coinciding with the times the medication was taken), and the other was that she found feelings hard to notice and express. The best and easiest way to accommodate these factors is simply to ask and negotiate a way of working together that takes them into account. I never assume I know what someone needs; I am generally wrong if I do.

The reverse side of this is my firm belief that, when working with frail people, we can find a balance between treading carefully and providing an environment where challenge and active discourse can happen. Remember that moment with Kate that I almost instantly regretted? If we engage in surface level, inauthentic 'idle chatter' (van Deurzen, 2002), we are missing the magic of what happens when two people really meet. If we notice what is happening in the here and now between us and the other people in the room, we have the chance to open our awareness and see more clearly how life is for them. It was my experience of the disconnect between Bobby's charm and care and his narrative that he was mean that got us into exploring his inner life. We wouldn't have arrived there if I had been careful of him or pitied him. This balance, I believe, comes through building a strong therapeutic alliance. It obviously needs to be considered alongside what is ethically right, and this, in my opinion, is where supervision can be helpful. My plea is that we all consider when we might be filtering or making allowances based on our own perceptions of a client's weakness, which may not be what is experienced by our client and may not preclude normal courses of action.

Listen to life stories

As we approach our old age, we face almost constant change, logistically, biologically, neurologically and psychologically. One way to find meaning and order within this is to tell stories. Our customs, history and identity have been kept alive over the centuries by word of mouth, in the form of storytelling. It is also a way of protecting identity and subverting outside influences when under attack from others, and a way of making sense of our place in the world.

So, as we age and cope with change, retelling our life stories is one way of protecting and also continuing to evolve our own identity. Practically, whether with the onset of dementia symptoms or simply as a result of our ageing brain, our short-term memory normally begins to falter ahead of our long-term memory. Not remembering something can be frightening; therefore, it can be reassuring to recollect memories. The easiest way to engage with this is to look through photos with someone, to prompt memories of early family life, friends and school experiences. Be curious. A powerful way to honour and confirm someone is to listen to their story (Slater, 1995). This isn't about sentimentalising the stories; it is about hearing them and having them heard. Often they will subtly change and evolve, even if retold many times, and these changes and shifts will hold something powerful within them. Like the moment Maggie, in Chapter 1, told me she got married the previous week and that her late husband was happy for her. True, or untrue, the account was rich with meaning.

As I wrote in the introduction to this book, Erikson, when adding the final life stage to his theory of human development, suggested that reflecting on and reaching acceptance of the life that has been lived are among the key tasks of ageing well (Erikson & Erikson, 1998). This process is part of attaining wisdom, of locating oneself within time and within generations. It is also a powerful rebellion against the stories that other people tell us. Wider society tends to generalise, whether in relation to gender, race, age, sexual orientation, disability or any other broad category. I have explored frequently in this book the many ways in which older adults are stereotyped. Telling stories, and having them listened to, is a wonderful way of celebrating and retaining our own, unique identity. So, sit, be curious and listen as these stories are told and retold.

Meet people where they are

When supporting or working alongside people who are profoundly old and retreating into their inner world, or those with dementia or cognitive impairment who may not always appear to have a grasp on what we might consider reality to be (and here I choose my words deliberately), I would urge you to stay in the reality that appears to be happening for the person you are with. It can be frightening to be told something isn't real or to be forced to engage with something external and strange, and it can mean that we are not walking alongside the other person. So, when Tom told me he was waiting for a bus, we waited for the bus together in the corridor of his nursing home. When Maggie was so still and introspective that she seemed to be sleeping, I sat quietly with her and merely reassured her of my presence. When she told me that she had got married the previous week, I didn't question it. When an incongruous word comes out, I don't correct it; instead, I invite the client to tell me more about its meaning. If we move on, correct or ignore, we lose vital opportunities to connect and, possibly, vital clues to the inner world of the other person.

Be flexible and expect the unexpected

My learning from working with older adults is that the unexpected and unplanned tend to happen quite regularly. If you are visiting someone in their home, you have to expect friends or family members to drop by, or a parcel to be delivered, or a ring-back from the doctor. As with

Cliff, if someone is being cared for in their own home, there are often interruptions from health visitors, drug deliveries and other services. With these clients, I generally check in our initial session when these interruptions are likely to happen and work our times around them. I also try to agree in the contracting process what we will do if we are interrupted. There is also the likelihood, as we saw earlier, that medication or medical conditions may impose some restrictions on the work.

Working with clients who are living in residential and nursing care homes can be equally unpredictable. As a general rule, I let the service manager know who I am and when I will be visiting a client and I also try to ring ahead on the day of the session. This is for several reasons. I have, more than once, arrived to find the person I am due to meet is having their hair done, watching a musical performance, out on a day trip or gone to see the GP – even, as with Tom, died – and no one has let me know. There is also a high likelihood that, even if you have requested privacy, care staff will come into the room to offer tea, give medicine or ask how things are. You have to be patient, creative and flexible about this, and try to hold onto a sense of humour. Supervision is a wonderful place to vent frustration and find practical solutions.

Don't objectify – challenge social constructs

One of the best pieces of advice I was given by a colleague about avoiding the archetype of 'elderly' was to ask to see photos of the client when they were younger. This is for no other reason than to remind yourself that the person before you, who may be hunched over, with whitened hair, unable to walk, has an identity and life that transcends what you can see before you with your own eyes. Objectification of social and cultural groups is all around us; it is largely inescapable. Our job is to be aware of stereotypes and work to find and experience the particular, unique identity of the person before us. The easiest way to close the gap between observer and observed is to be curious, to ask, to hold the space for stories and accounts to be told, to be reflective about how you feel in relation to this person, and then to explore this together (Karpen, cited in Wyatt-Brown, Ray & Kivnick, 2016).

I was very nervous about writing this book, as I knew I would have to make some general statements that, by their very nature, would move us away from the idiographic. In my work, I find that supervision allows me to notice if I am generalising or objectifying. I can tell it is happening when I make broad statements or begin to lean too heavily on theory. These two things naturally take me further from the uniqueness of the person. One very effective way of noticing if you are objectifying someone is if their age and aspects of ageing are the only things you explore in supervision (Rapp, 2000), as it suggests that this is all you can see. I believe it is essential to pause reflectively in supervision and check if I am filtering anything, notice what I am not saying and play close attention to the language I use.

I also find it useful to look for new research and ideas about our rapidly expanding ageing society. Much of this literature prompts me to look beyond stereotypes and challenge my own thinking. I have referenced some of this literature in the book – most significantly, Laura Carstensen's book, *A Long Bright Future* (2011), which summarises her years of research into happiness and longevity and smashes our suppositions about ageing. Another worth mentioning is Martinez's *The MindBody Code* (2016), which looks to centenarians for clues about happy longevity, focusing on biocognition. Another text that profoundly inspires me is, of course, Atul Gawande's work on dying, *Being Mortal* (2015), which challenges our misconceptions about this subject. These works, and many more like them, open new ways of thinking about life, advancing age and death, and I'd encourage anyone who seeks to work in this area to read widely and challenge their own views, no matter how progressive they think they are.

I want to end by encouraging all of us to age consciously and with curiosity, and to age in partnership with those around us. Venturing into older age and towards our death necessarily calls upon us to be introverted and reflective, but it also gives us license to be, stubbornly, all that we are and all that we can be, and for that we need others. Human beings are always in relation with each other. The power of humans to inspire and change each other is a miraculous thing. I offer this work to galvanise us all to live well and die well together.

References

Birren JE, Lubben JE, Rowe J C, and Deutchman DE (eds) (1991). *The Concept and Measurement of Quality of Life in the Frail Elderly*. San Diego, CA: Academic Press.

Bohart A, Tallman K (2010). Clients: the neglected common factor in psychotherapy. In: Duncan BL, Miller SD, Wampold BE, Hubble MA (eds). *The Heart and Soul of Change: delivering what works in therapy*. Washington, DC: American Psychological Association (pp83–111).

Carstensen L (2011). *A Long Bright Future*. New York, NY: Broadway Books.

Erikson EH, Erikson JM (1998). *The Life Cycle Completed*. New York, NY: WW Norton.

Gawande A (2015). *Being Mortal*. London: Profile Books.

Gilbert D (2014). *The Psychology of your Future Self*. [Online.] Ted2014. www.ted.com/talks/dan_gilbert_you_are_always_changing/ (accessed 9 November 2018).

Jung CG (1934/2014). The soul and death. In: Read H, Fordham M, Adler G (eds). *CG Jung: The Collected Works vol VIII*. Hove: Routledge (pp3360–3372).

MacDonald G (2017). Death in life or life in death? Dementia's ontological challenge. *Death Studies* 42(5): 290–297. doi: 10.1080/07481187.2017.1396398

Martinez M (2016). *The Mindbody Code: how to change the beliefs that limit your health, longevity, and success*. Louisville, CO: Sounds True Publishing.

Miller BJ (2015). *What Really Matters at the End of Life?* Ted2015. www.ted.com/talks/bj_miller_what_really_matters_at_the_end_of_life (accessed 9 November 2018).

Rapp H (2000). Working with difference. In: Lawton B, Feltham C (eds). *Taking Supervision Forward: enquiries and trends in counselling and psychotherapy*. London: Sage Publications (pp93–112).

Rogers CR (1980). Growing older – or older and growing. *Journal of Humanistic Psychology* 20(4): 6–16.

Sartre J-P (1943/2003). *Being and Nothingness: an essay on phenomenological ontology*. Abingdon: Routledge.

Slater R (1995). *The Psychology of Growing Old: looking forward*. Buckingham: Open University Press.

Van Deurzen E (2002). Heidegger's challenge of authenticity. In: du Plock S (ed). *Further Existential Challenges to the Psychotherapeutic Theory and Practice: papers from Existential Analysis*. London: Society for Existential Practice (pp370–379).

Wyatt-Brown AM, Ray RR, Kivnick HQ (2016). *The Big Move: life between the turning points*. Bloomington, IN: Indiana University Press.

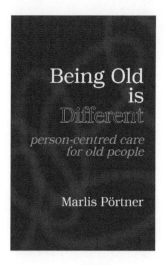

Being Old is Different:
person-centred care for old people
by Marlis Pörtner

PCCS Books

ISBN – 978 1 898059 99 8

Available from
www.pccs-books.co.uk

Marlis Pörtner's book is not about specific nursing or therapy methods but about fundamental principles, which are vital in many areas of care. The term 'carer', therefore, is used here for all those who, professionally or voluntarily, work with older people, and the term 'care' embraces nursing as well as family, therapeutic and supportive activities.

Being Old is Different describes some basic person-centred principles and their implementation in everyday care for the elderly. Marlis Pörtner, who describes herself as an old person, aims to demonstrate why the person-centred approach is particularly useful in this field; how it can be transferred into practice; how it helps to improve the life quality of older people and, at the same time, make work more satisfying for carers.

'[Marlis] writes with the insight and the authority of someone dedicated to the task of self-awareness and to the exercise of the idiosyncratic empathy which the kaleidoscopic range of elderly people who pass through the pages of her book demands. She is to be trusted because she so evidently practises what she preaches. Throughout the book colour and variety are added by the inclusion of telling vignettes which powerfully illustrate both the challenge and the beauty of those relationships which are crafted by a willingness on the part of the carers to refrain from diagnosis, impulsive reactions and rule-bound responses. I am encouraged by the example of Mr. L who at the age of 92 announced that he no longer wished to listen to the news during his breakfast. Clearly he had different business to attend to.'
Brian Thorne